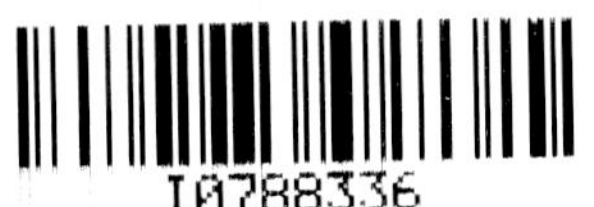

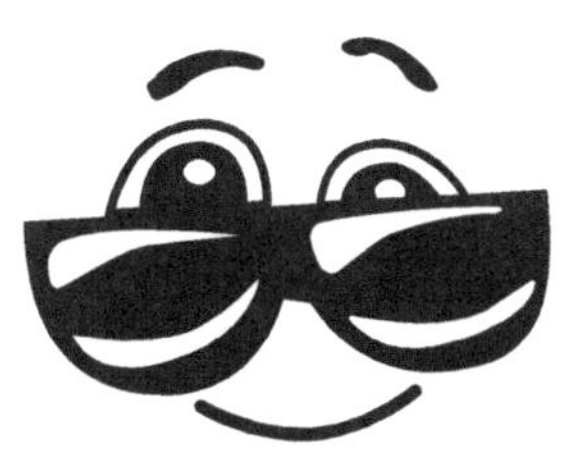

This coloring book belongs to :

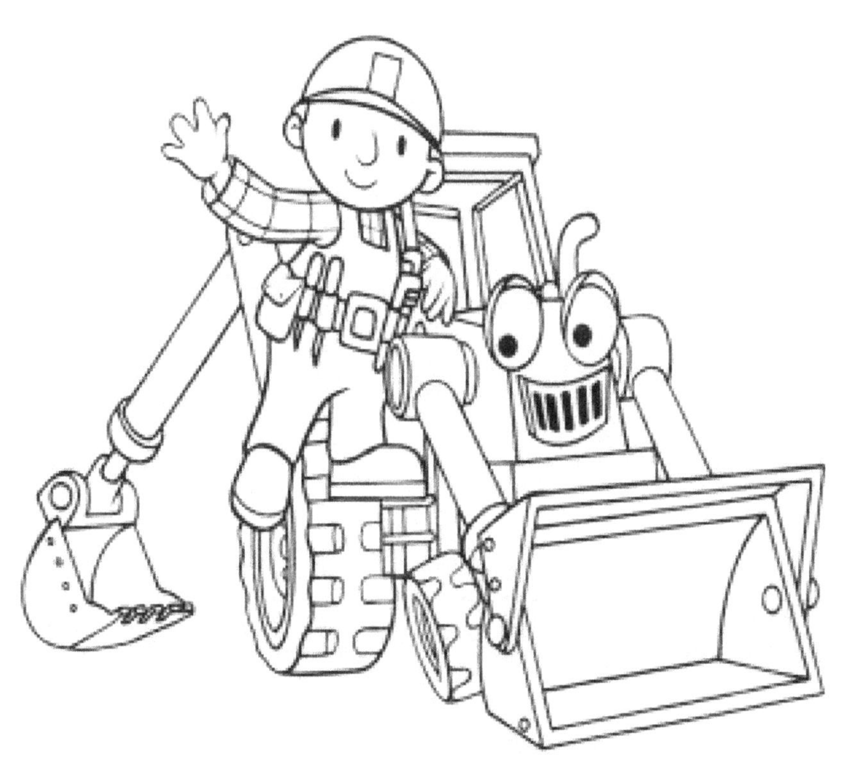

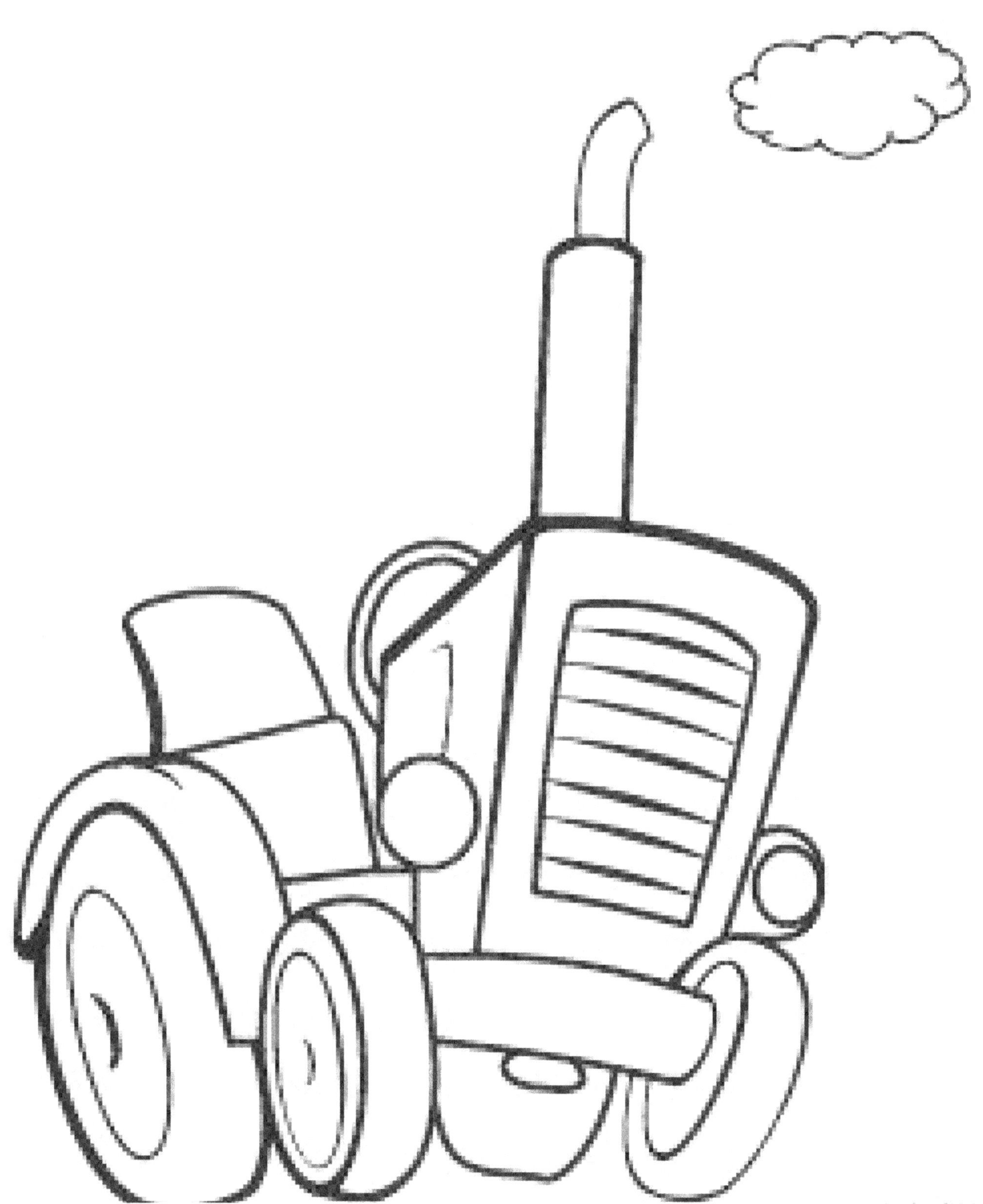

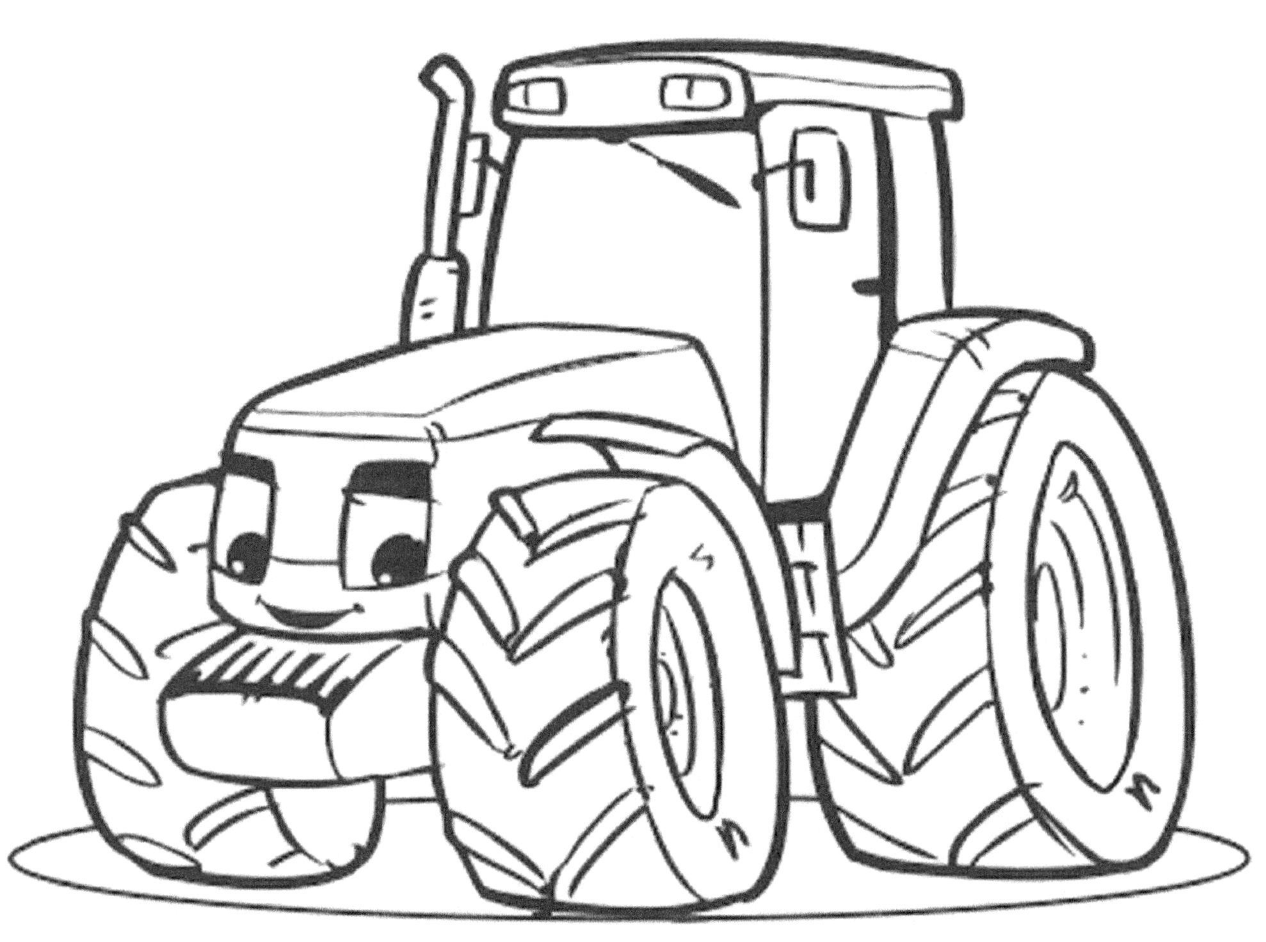

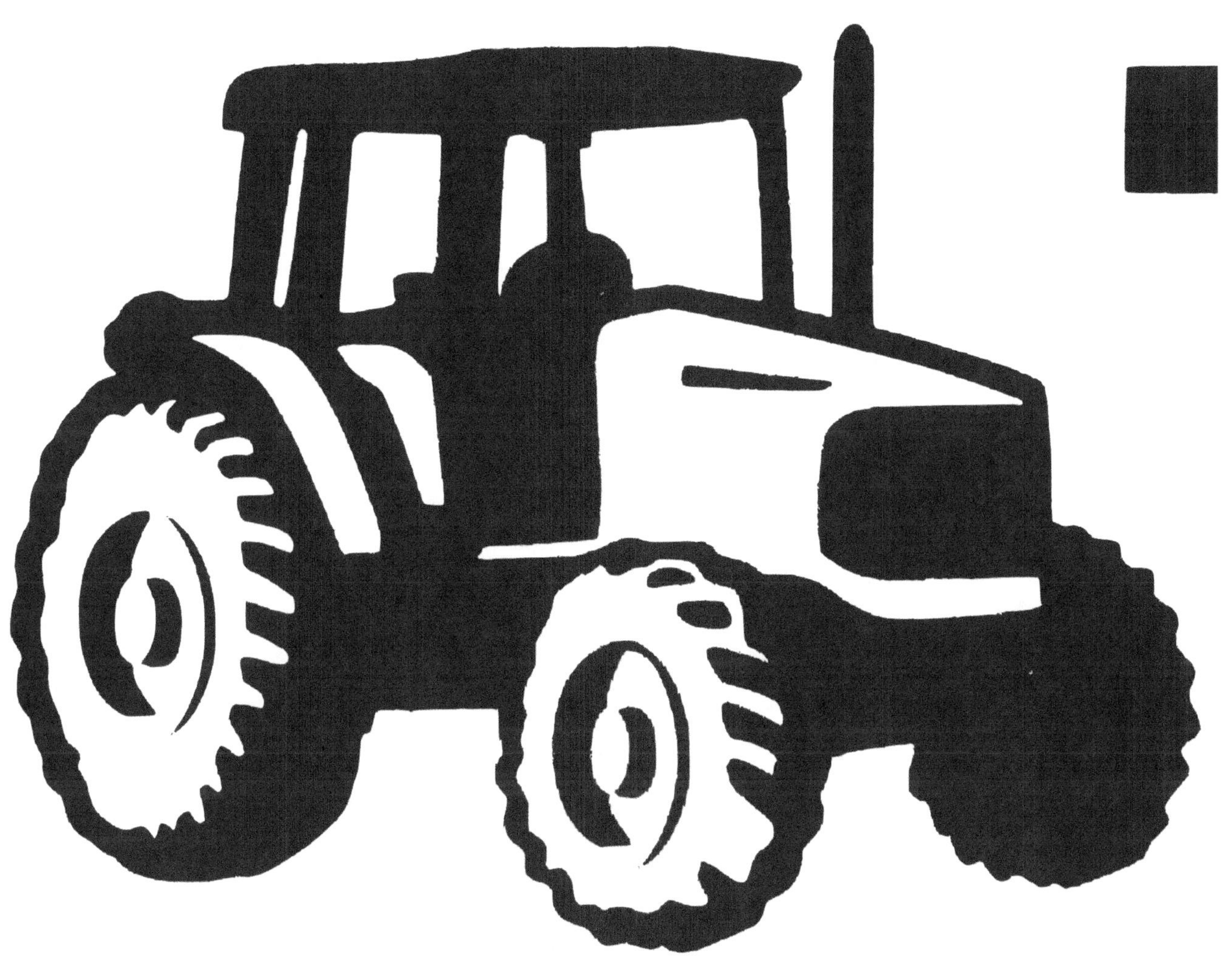

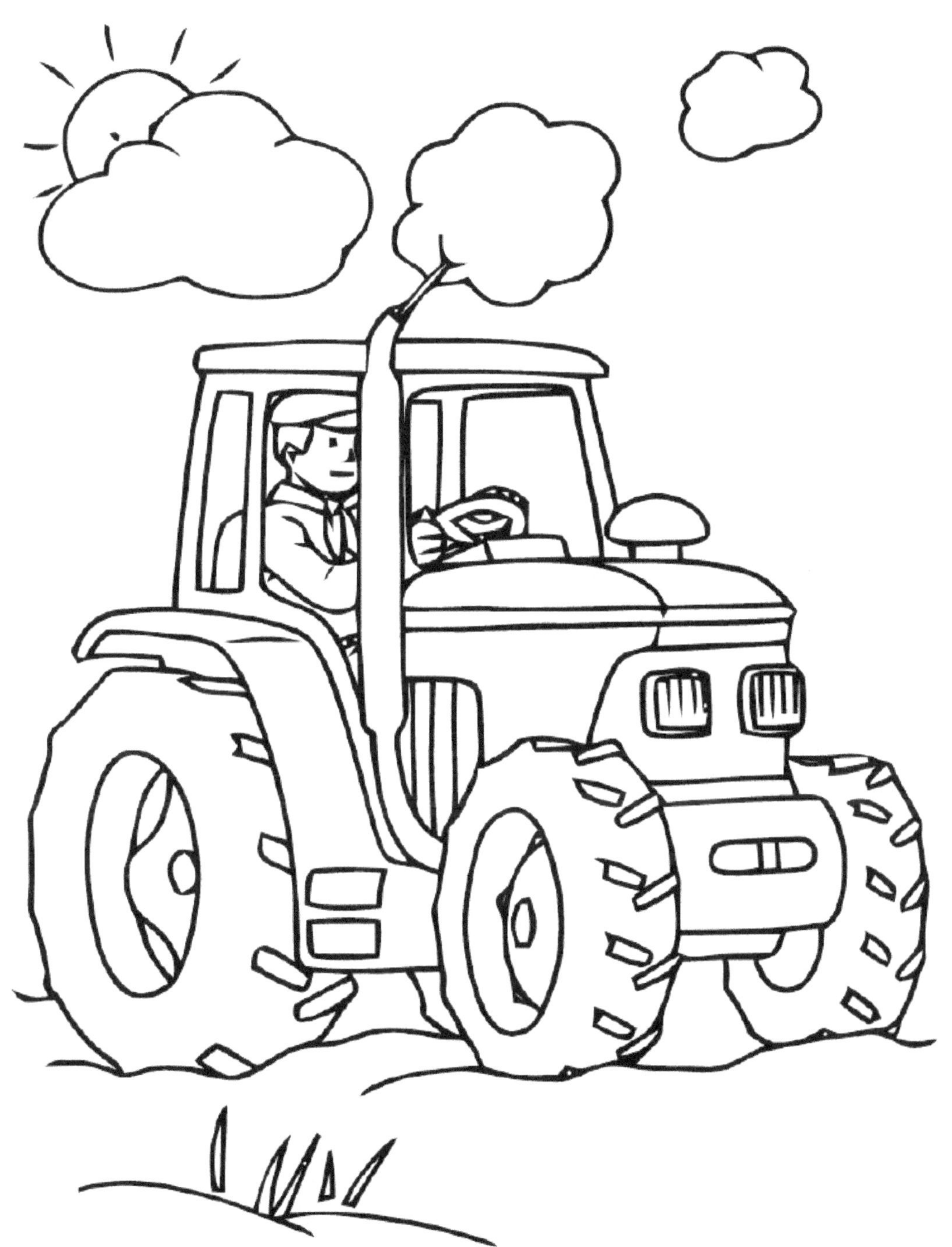

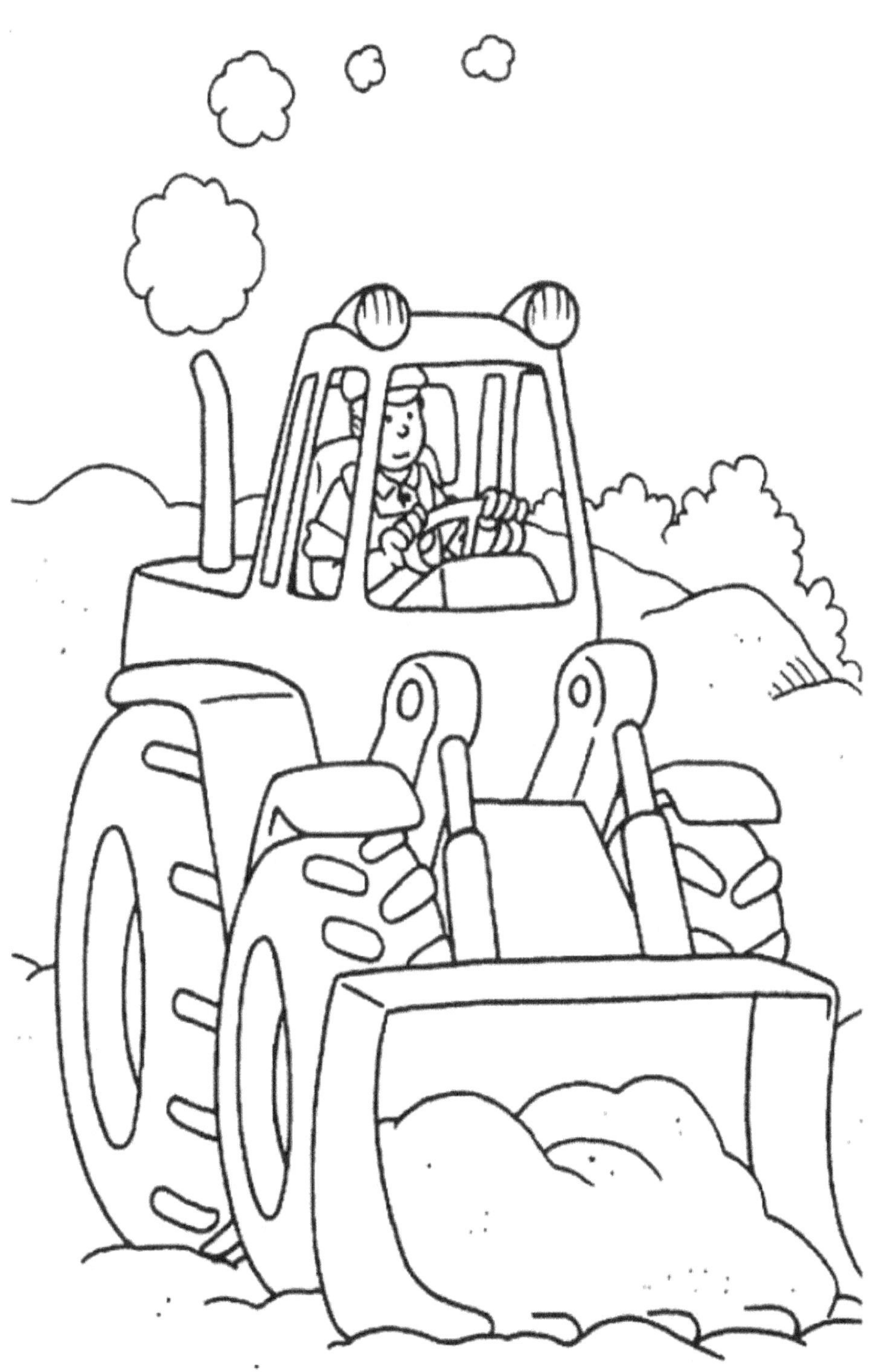

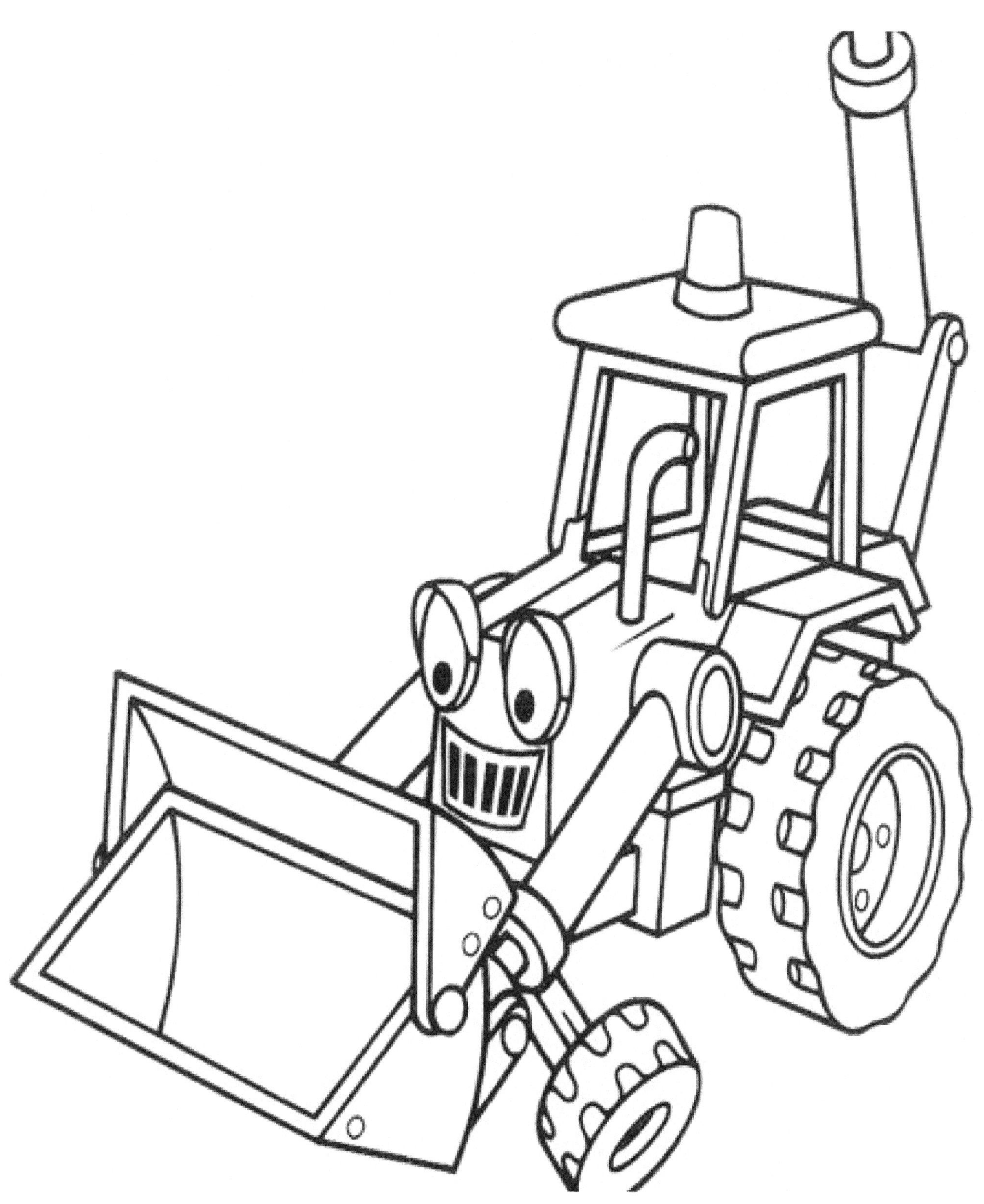

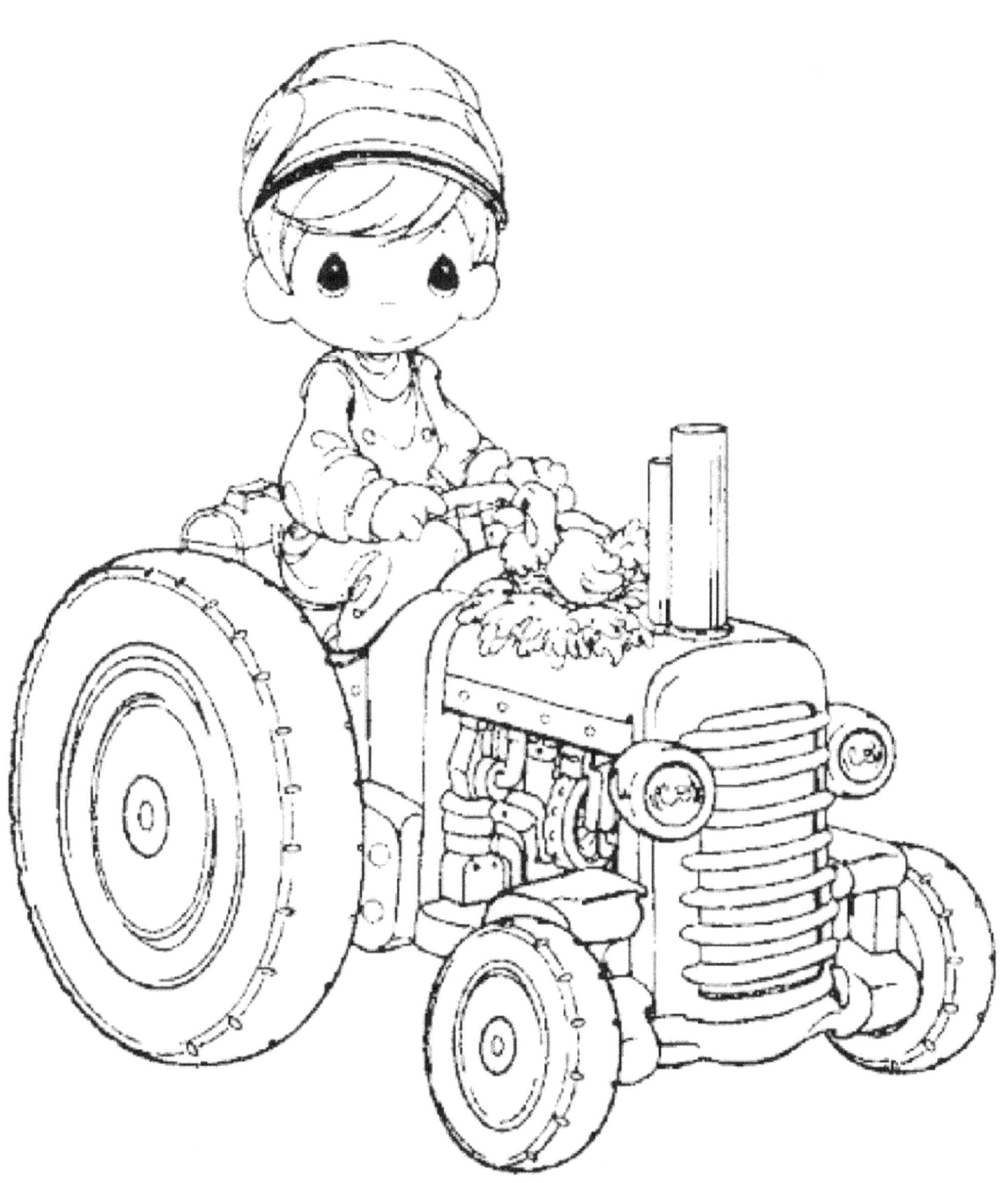

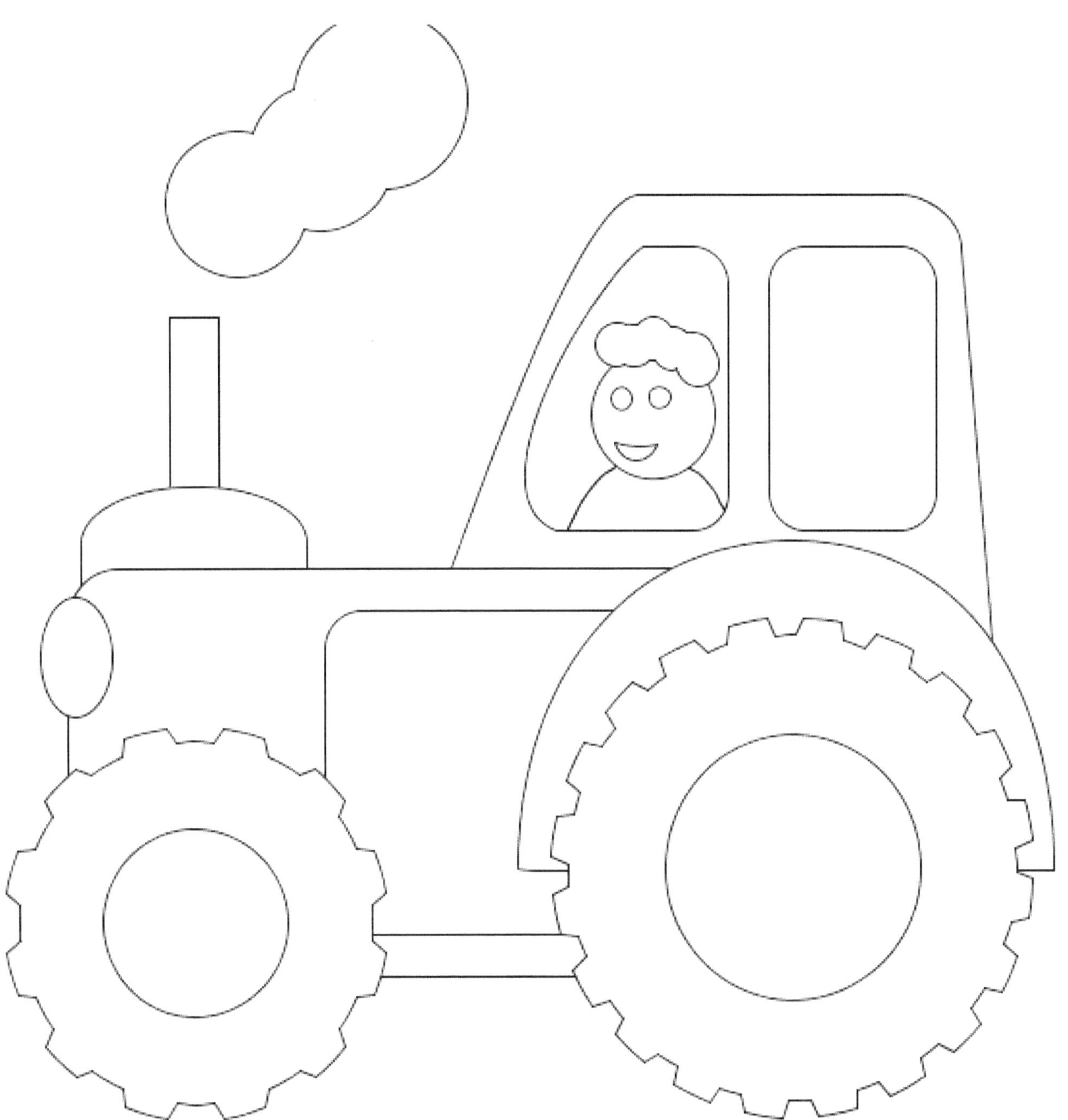

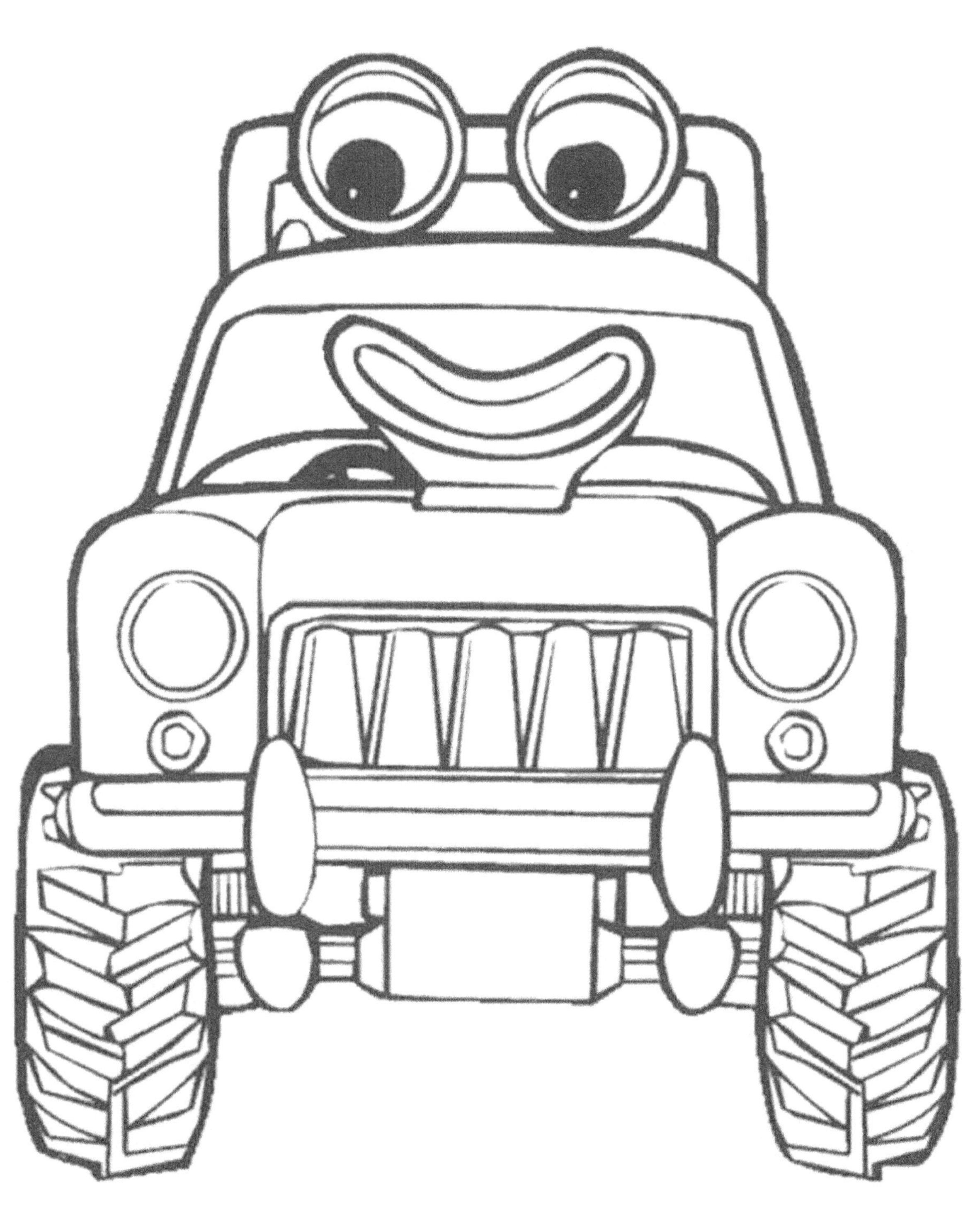

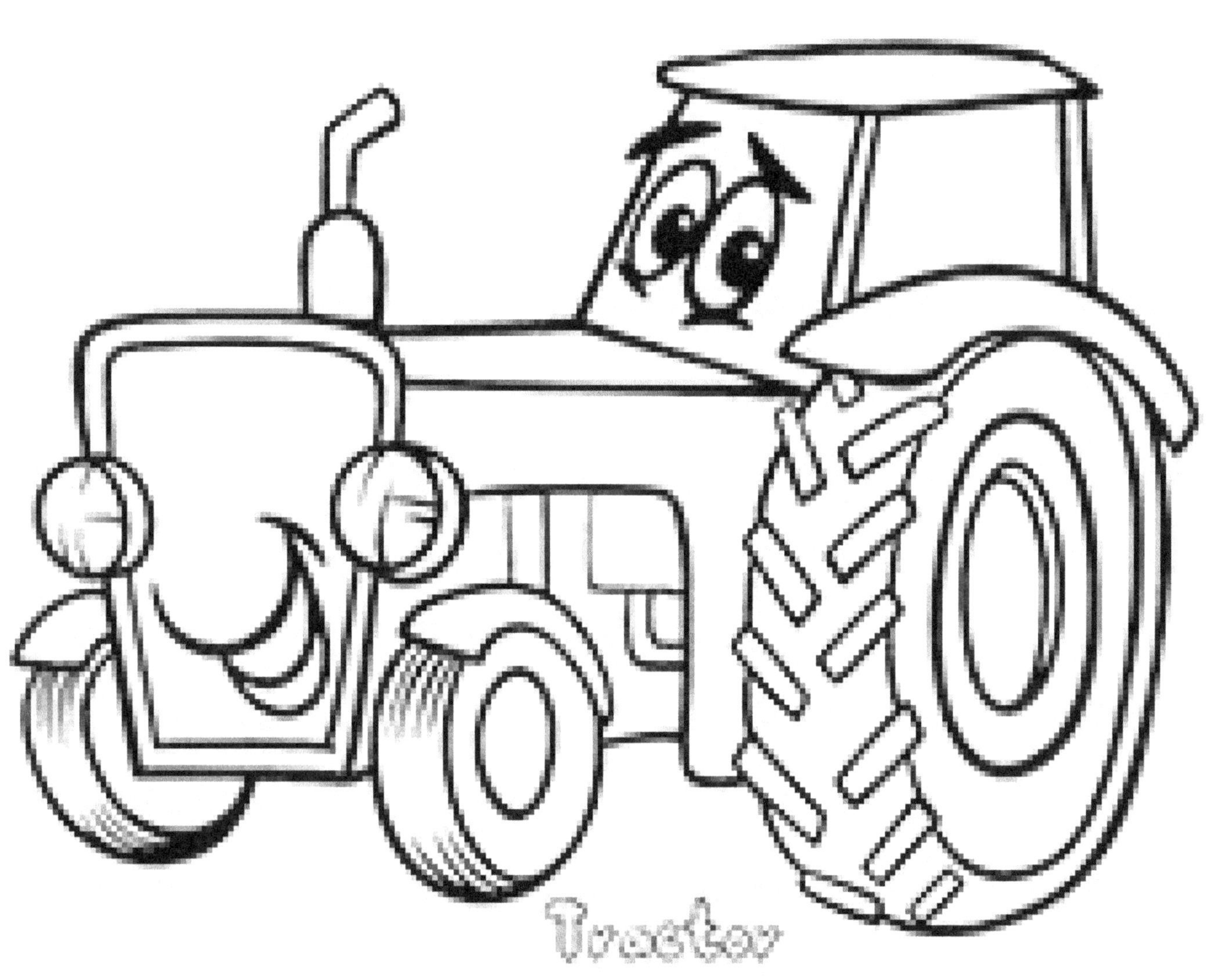
Tractor

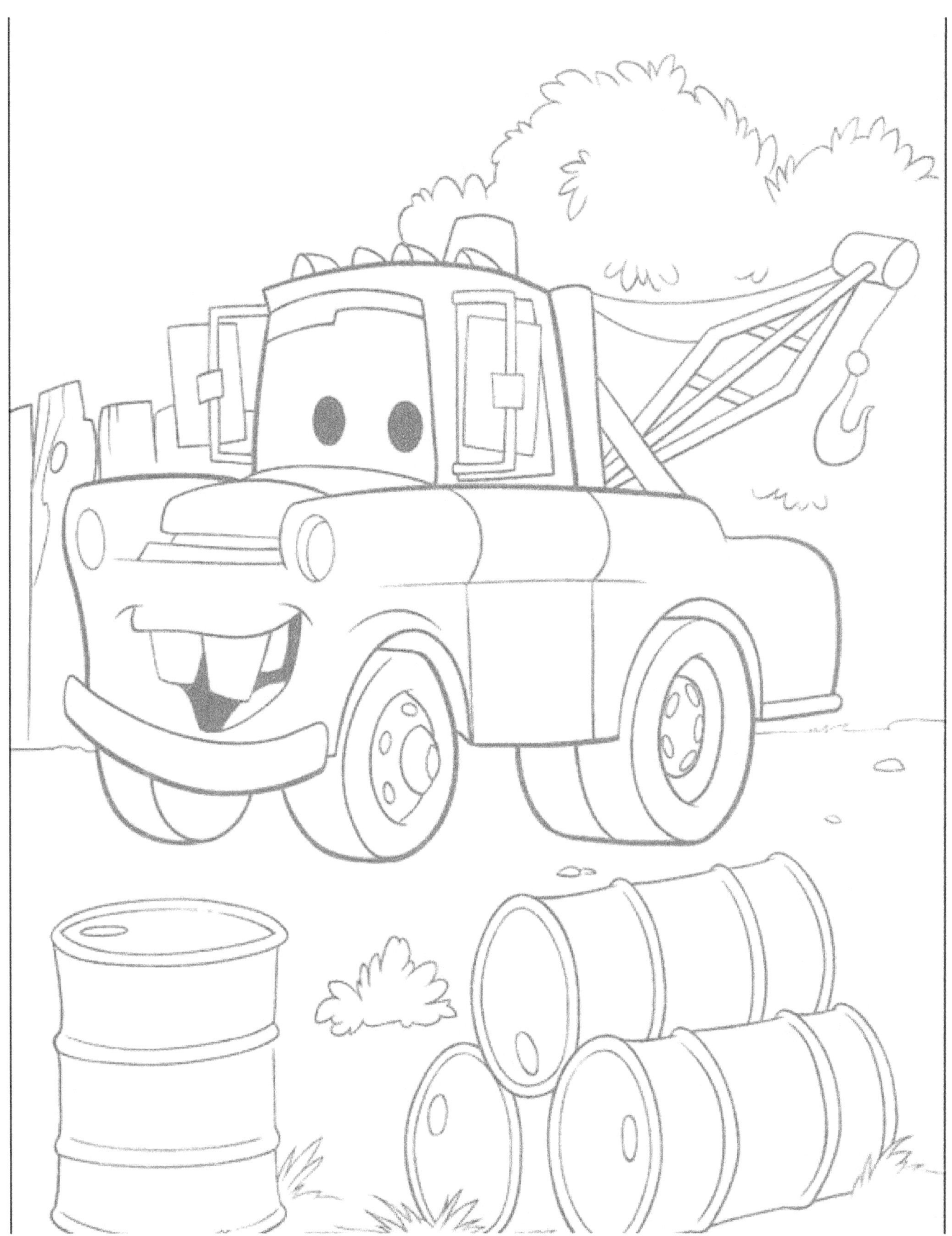

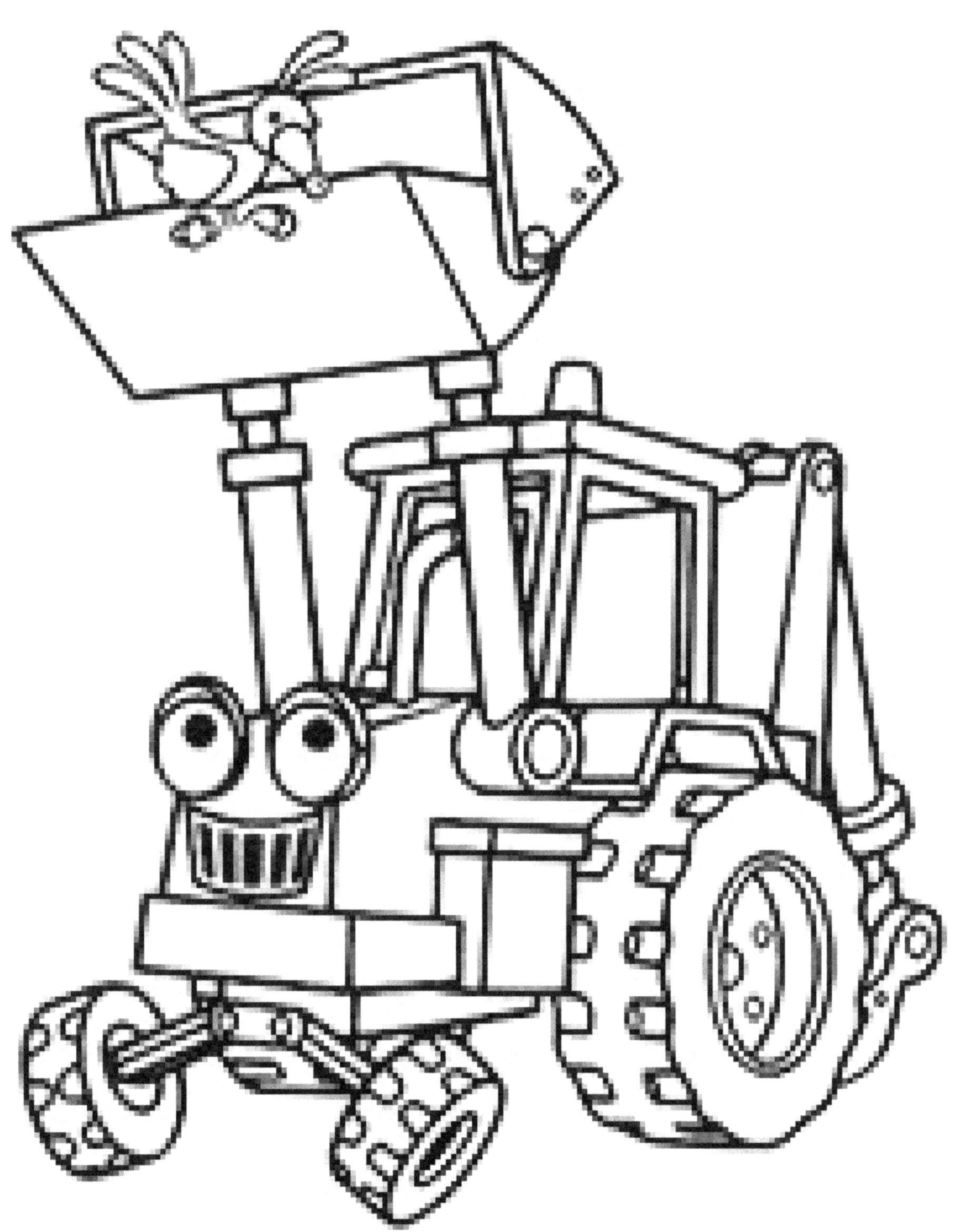

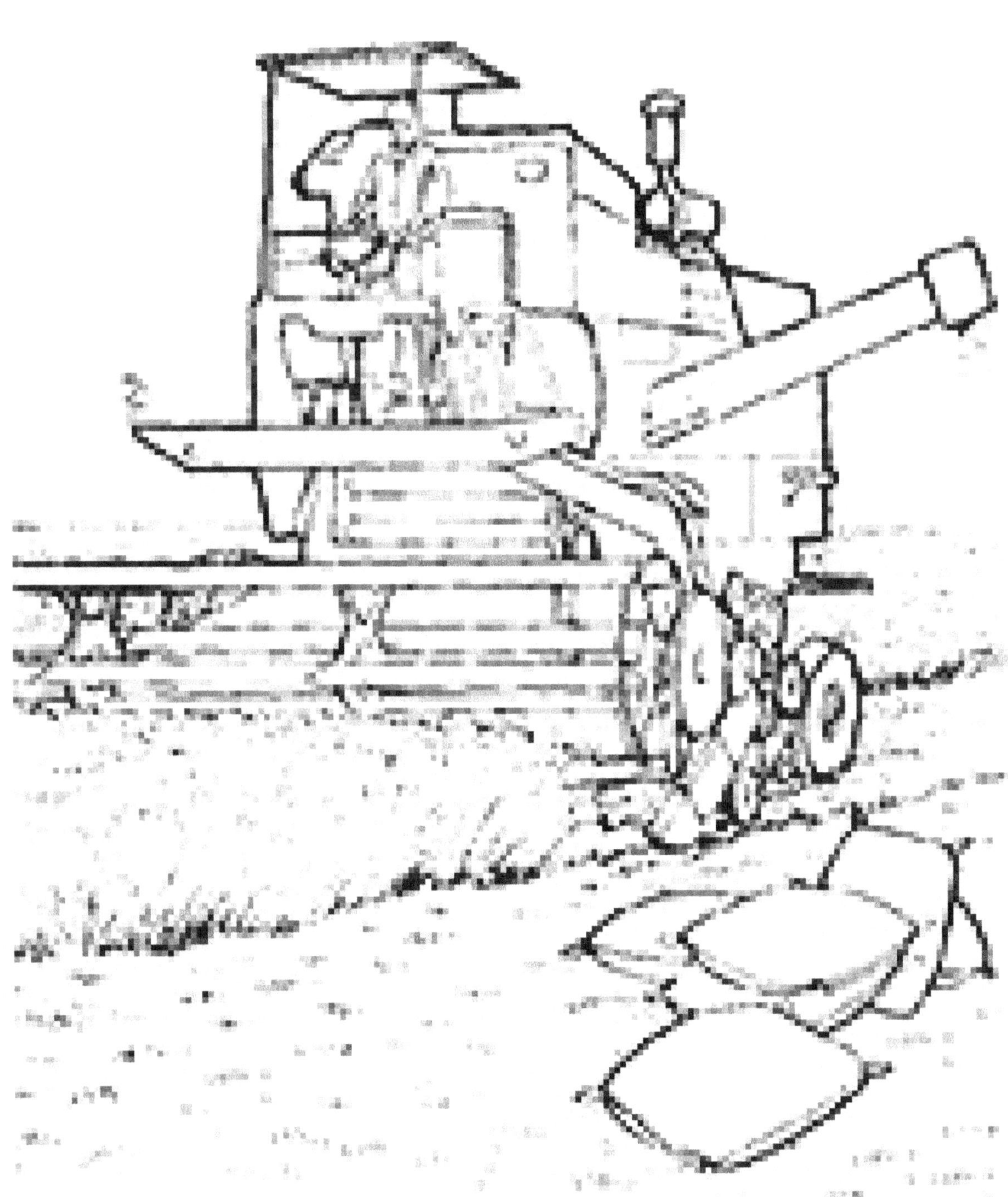

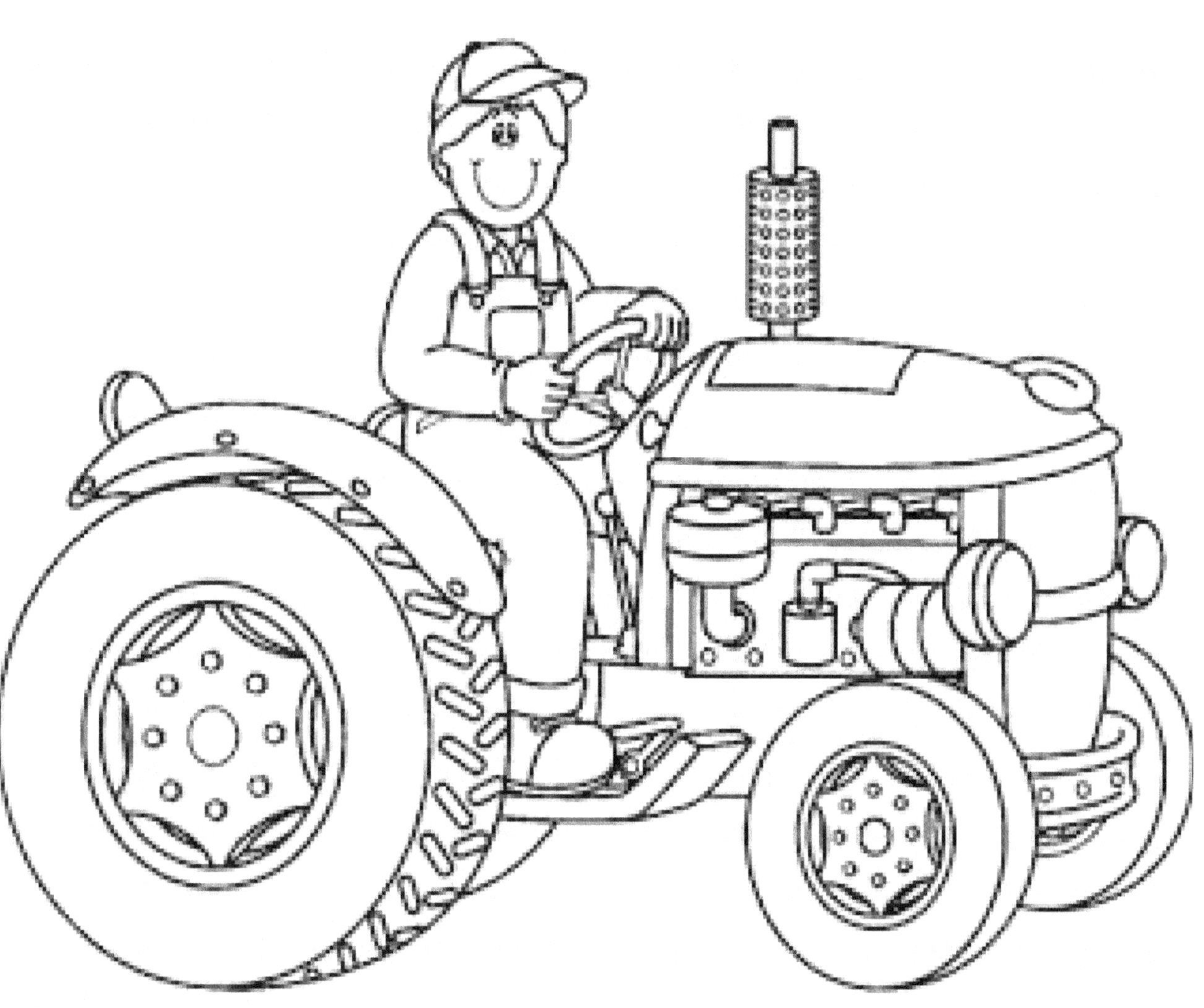

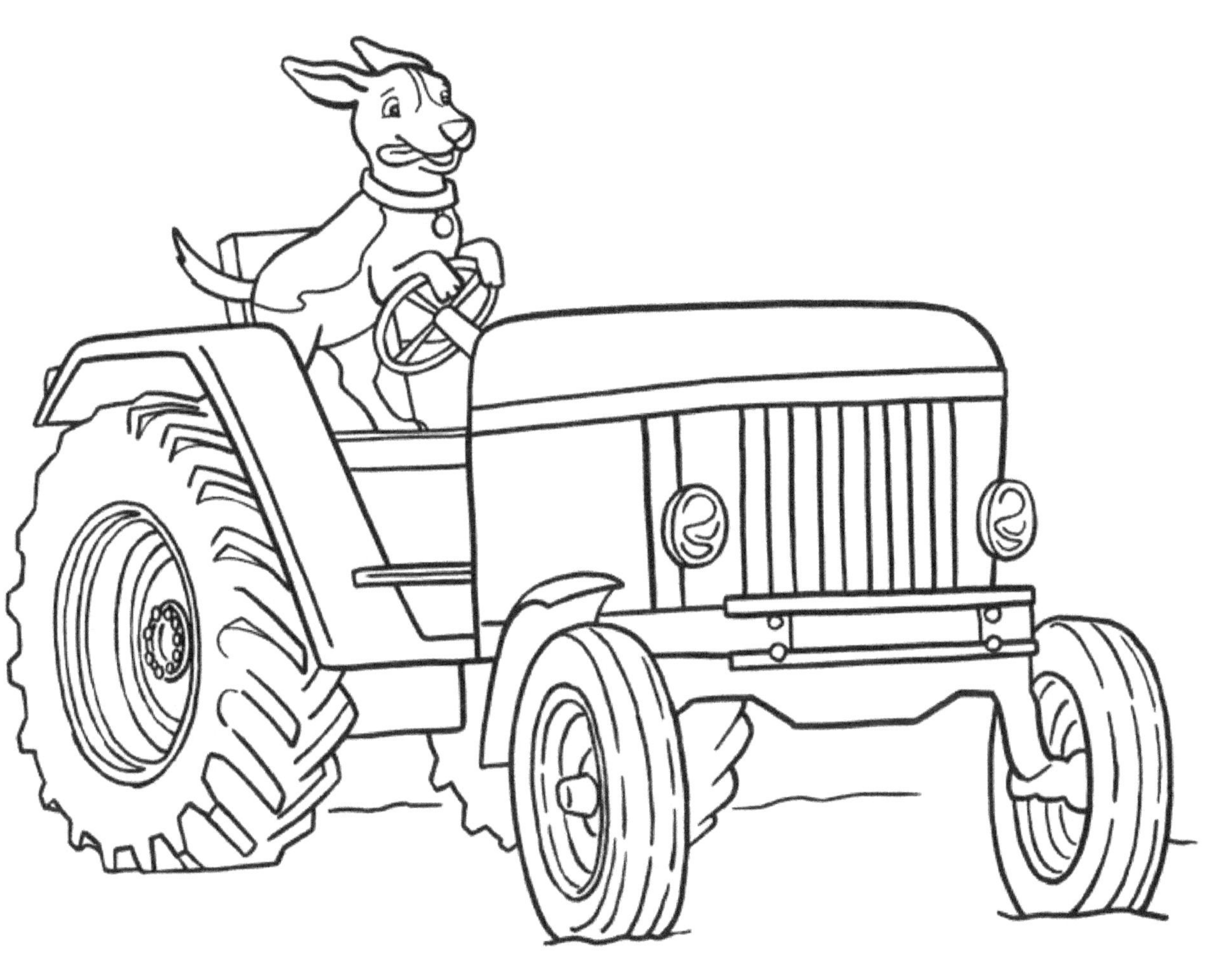

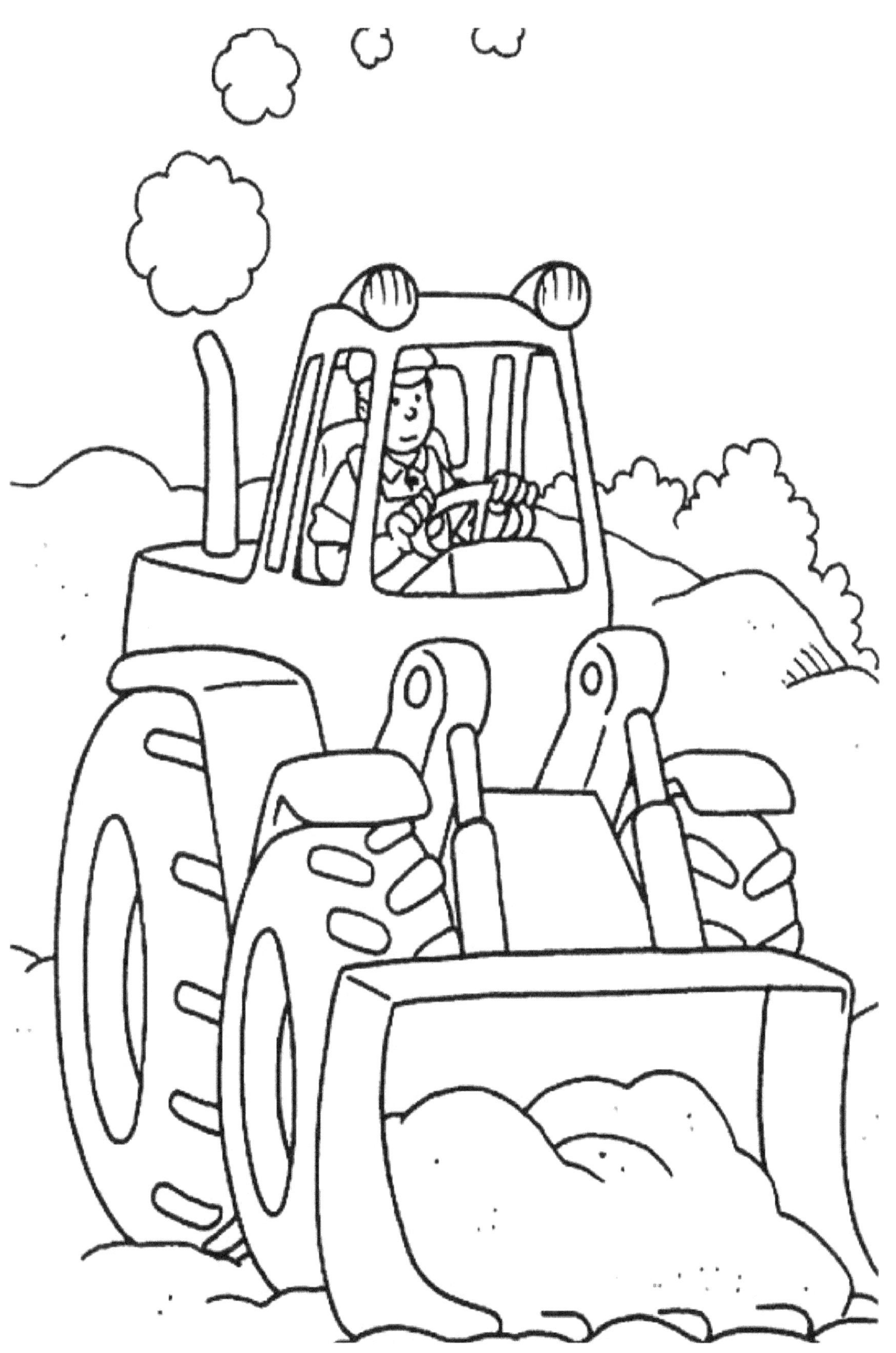

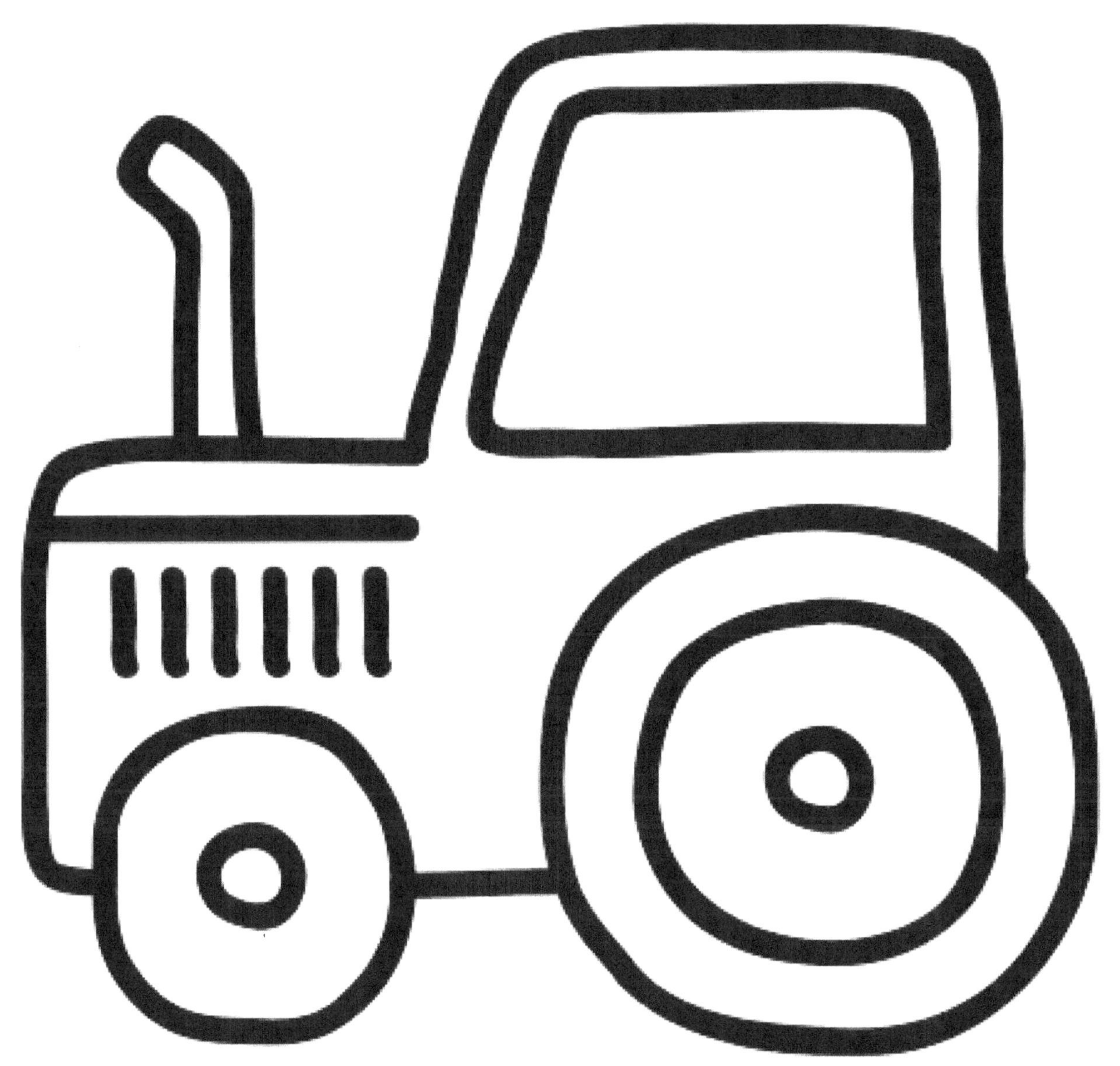

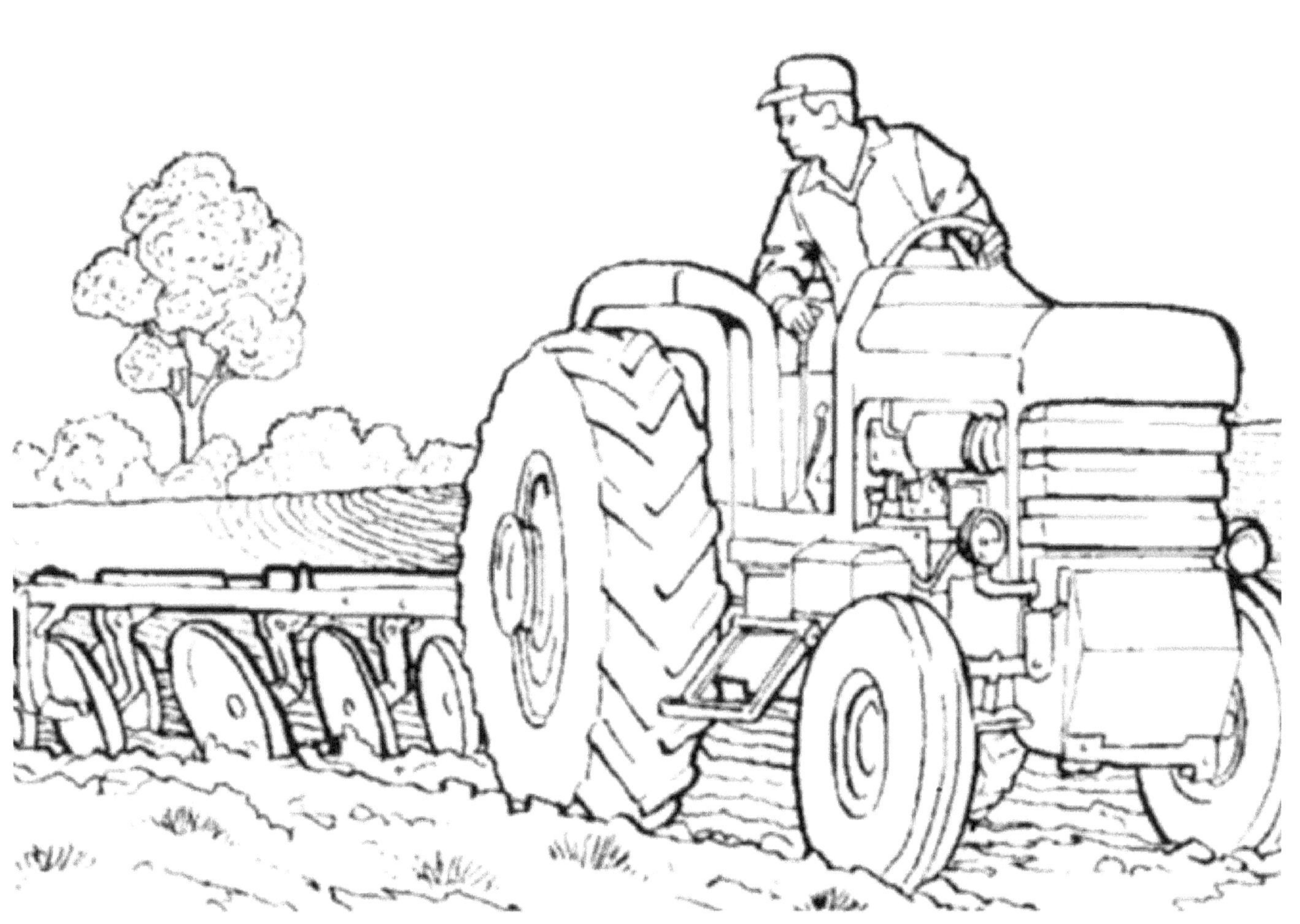

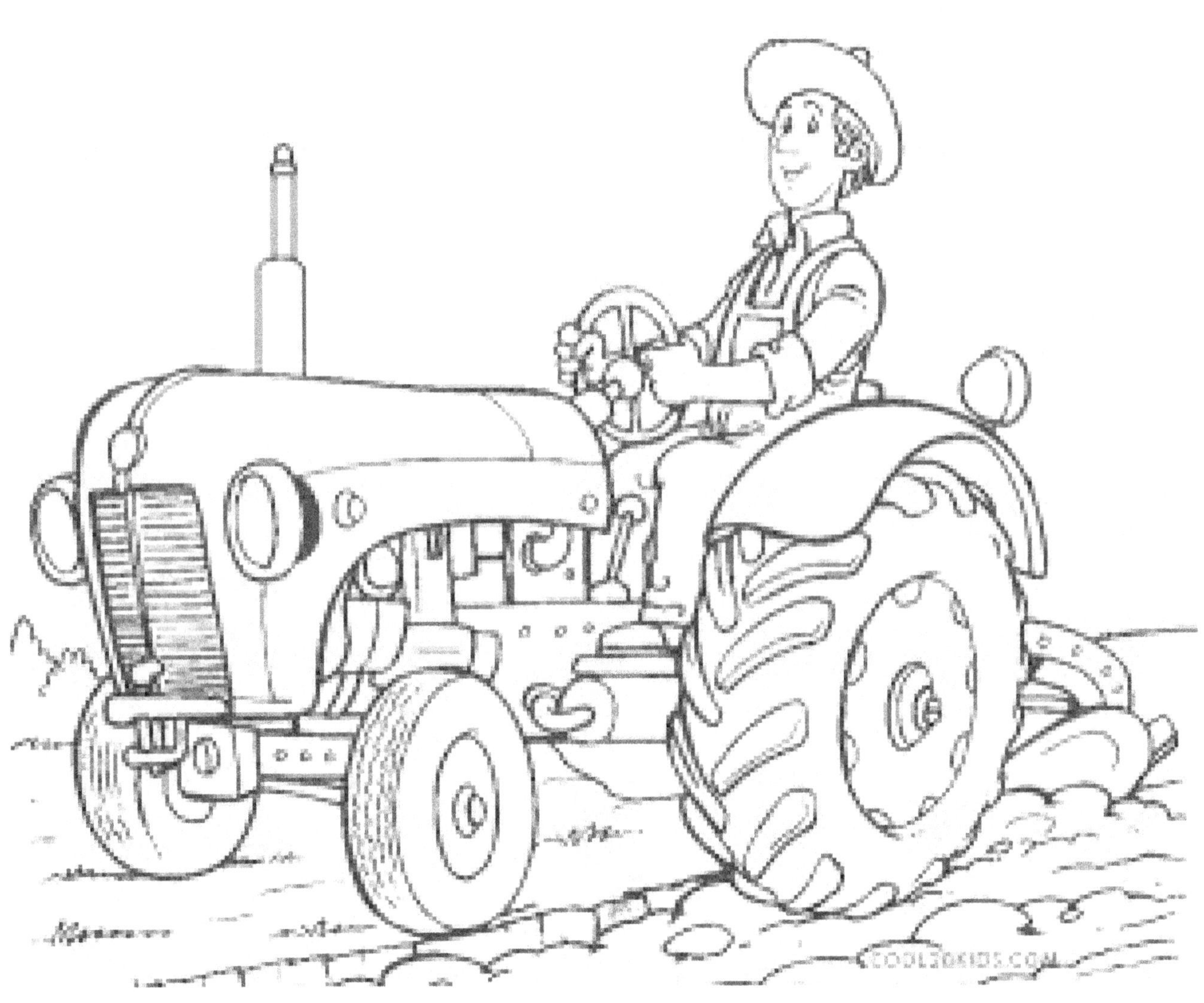

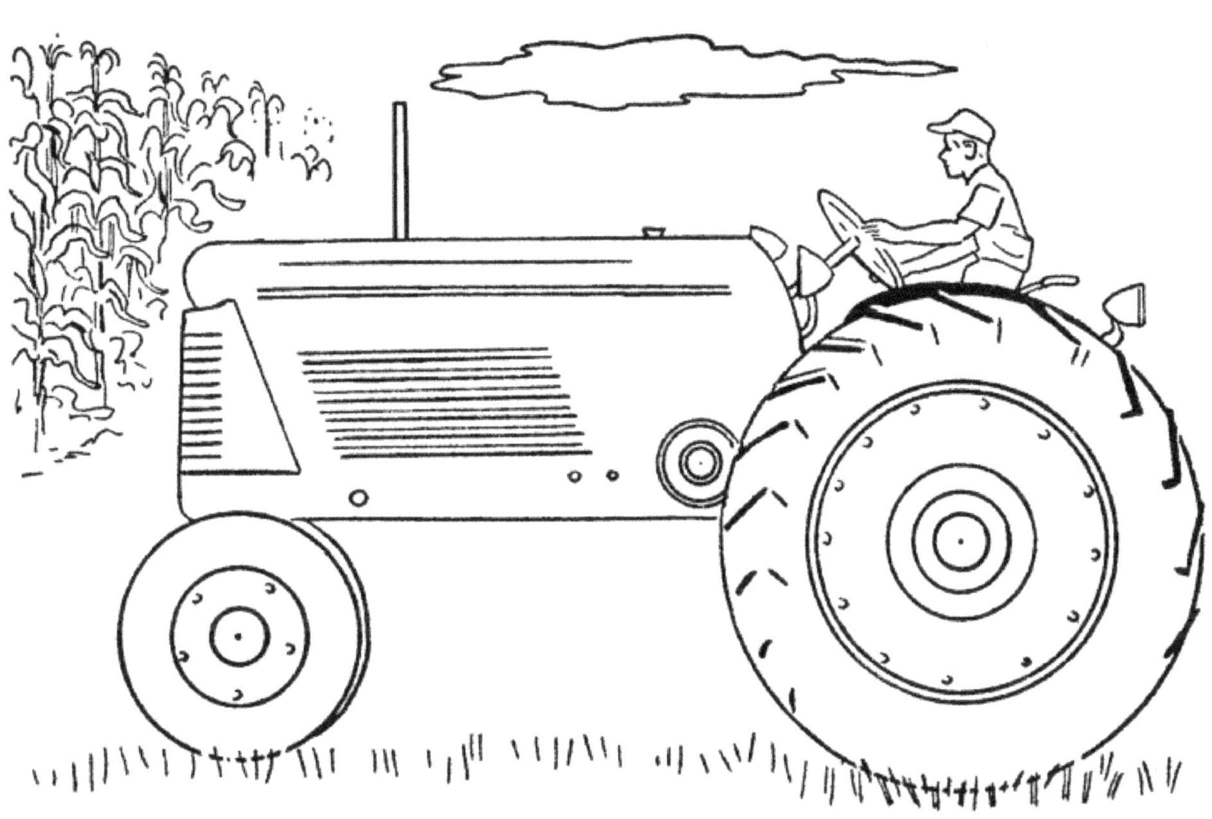

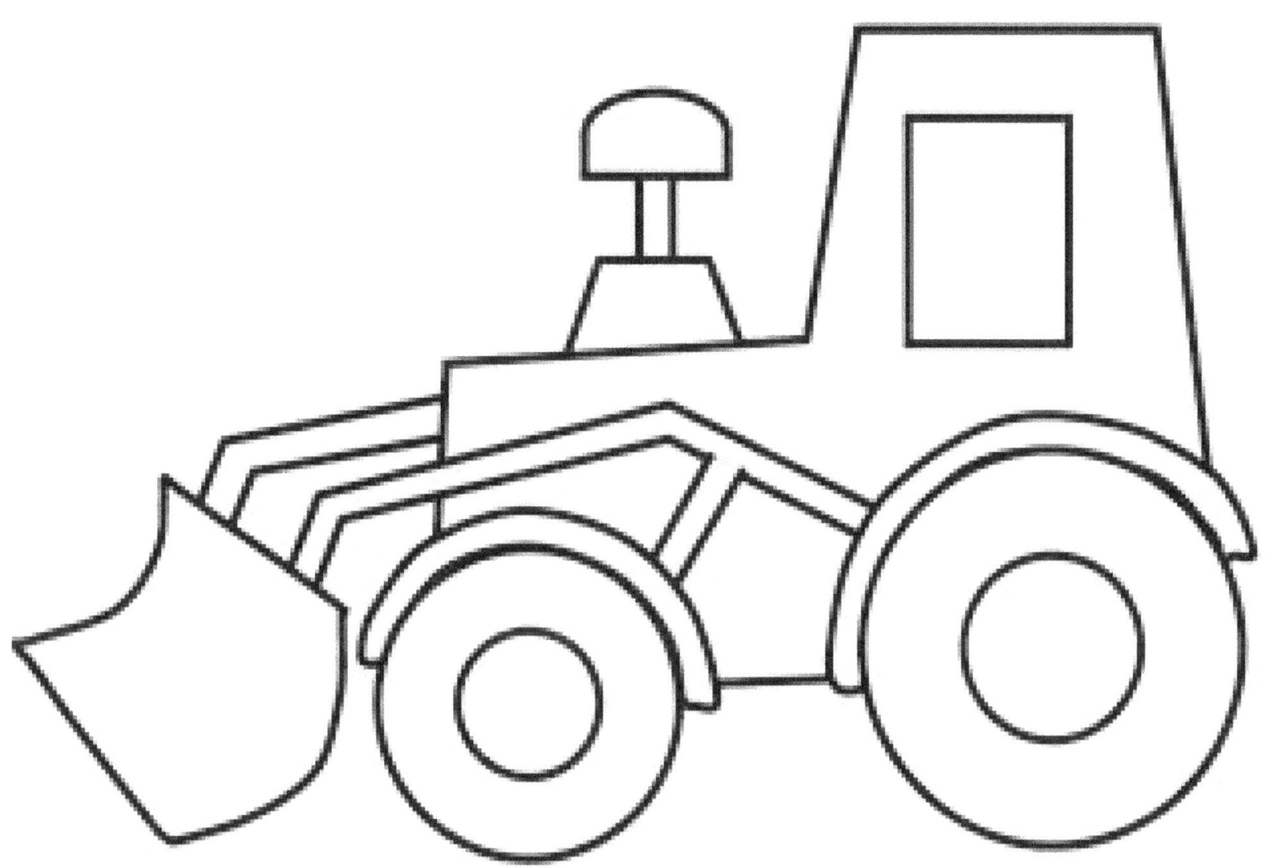

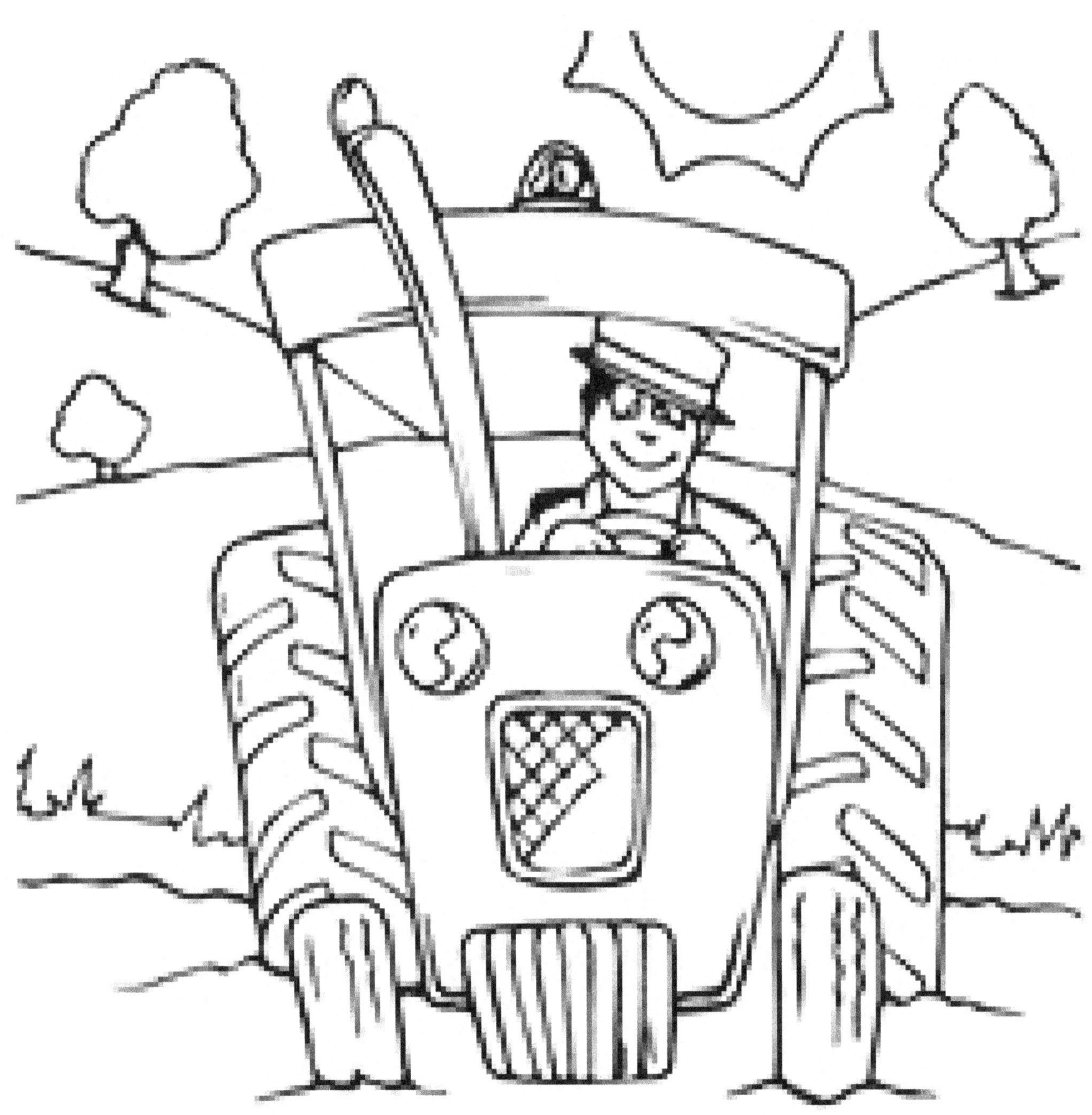

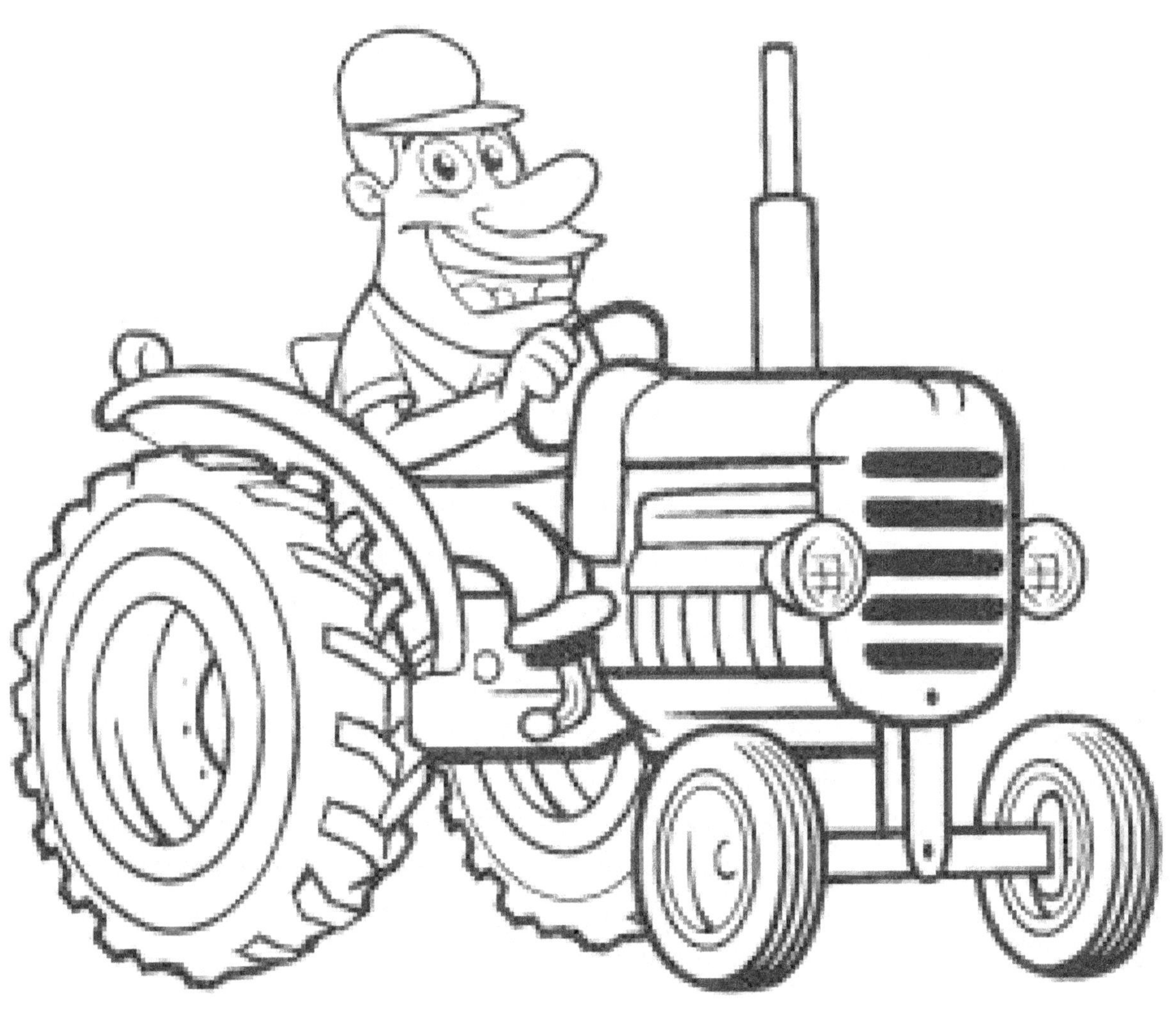

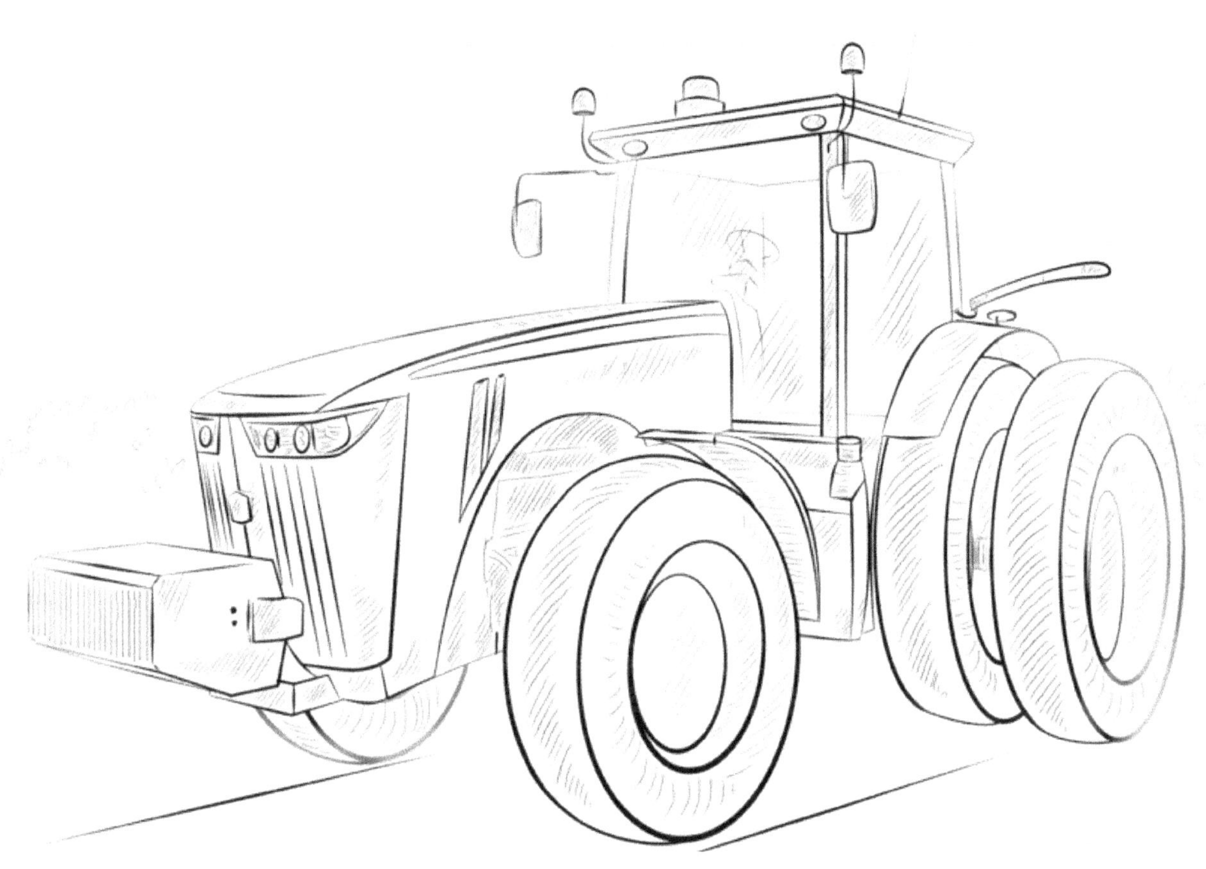

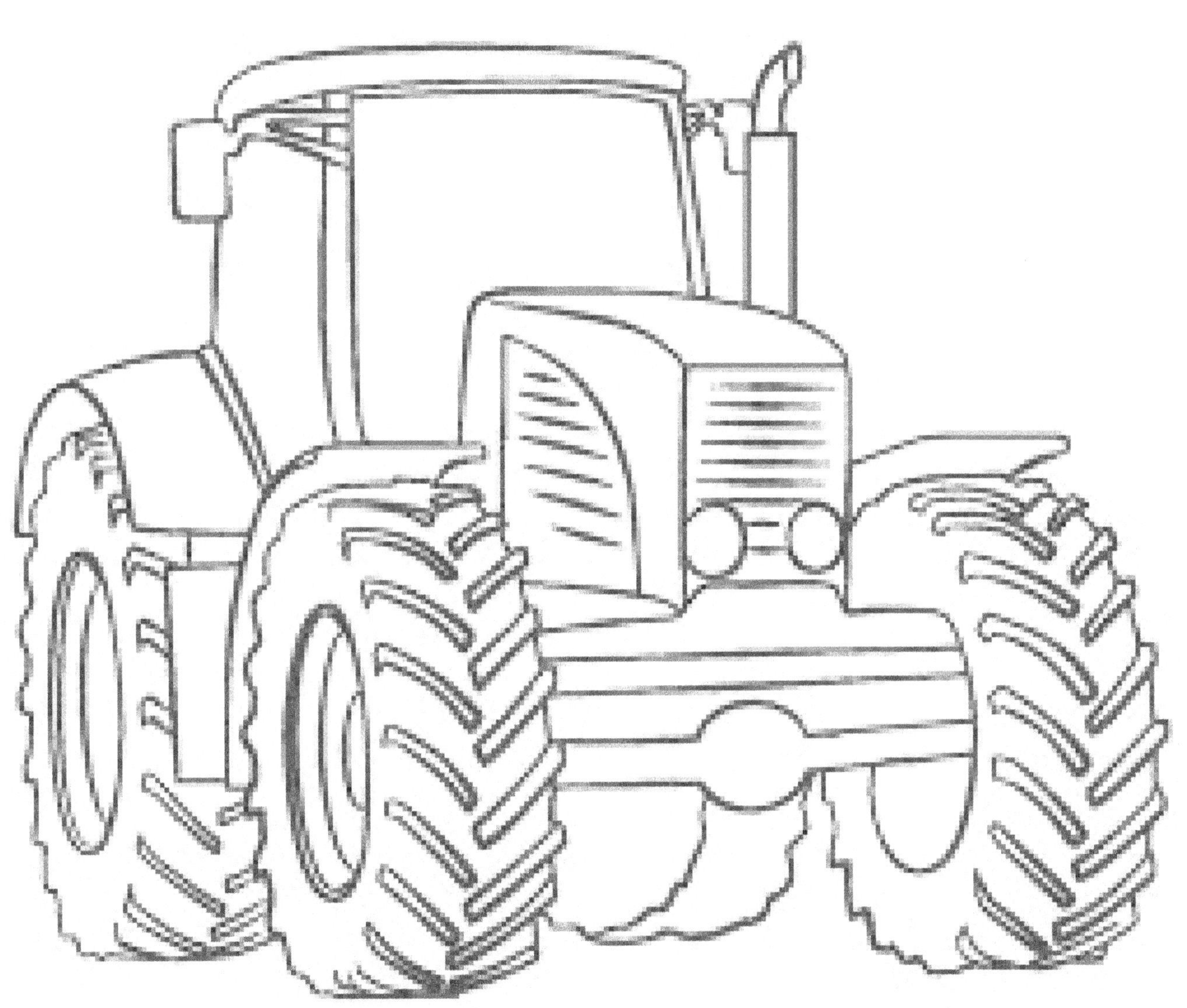

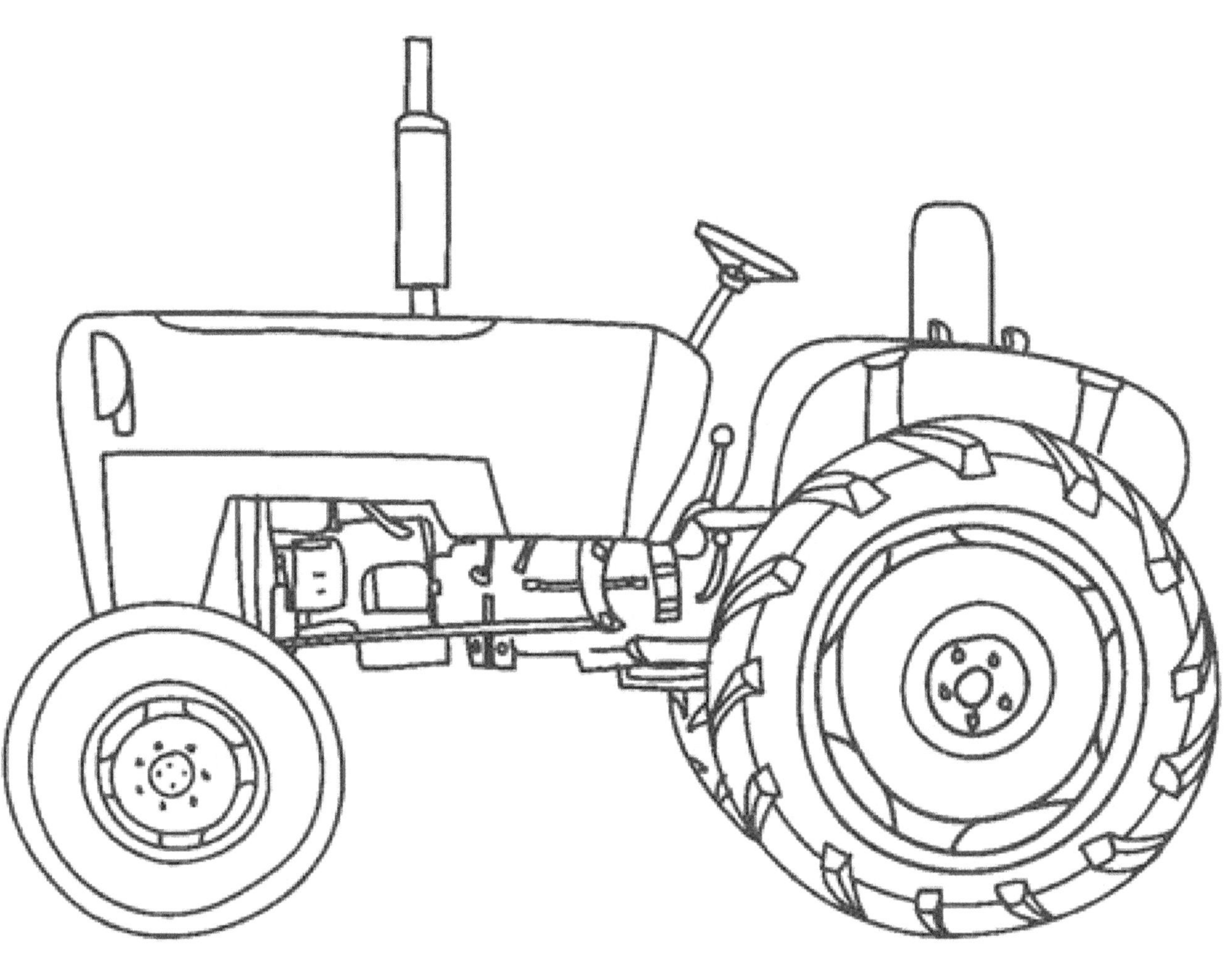

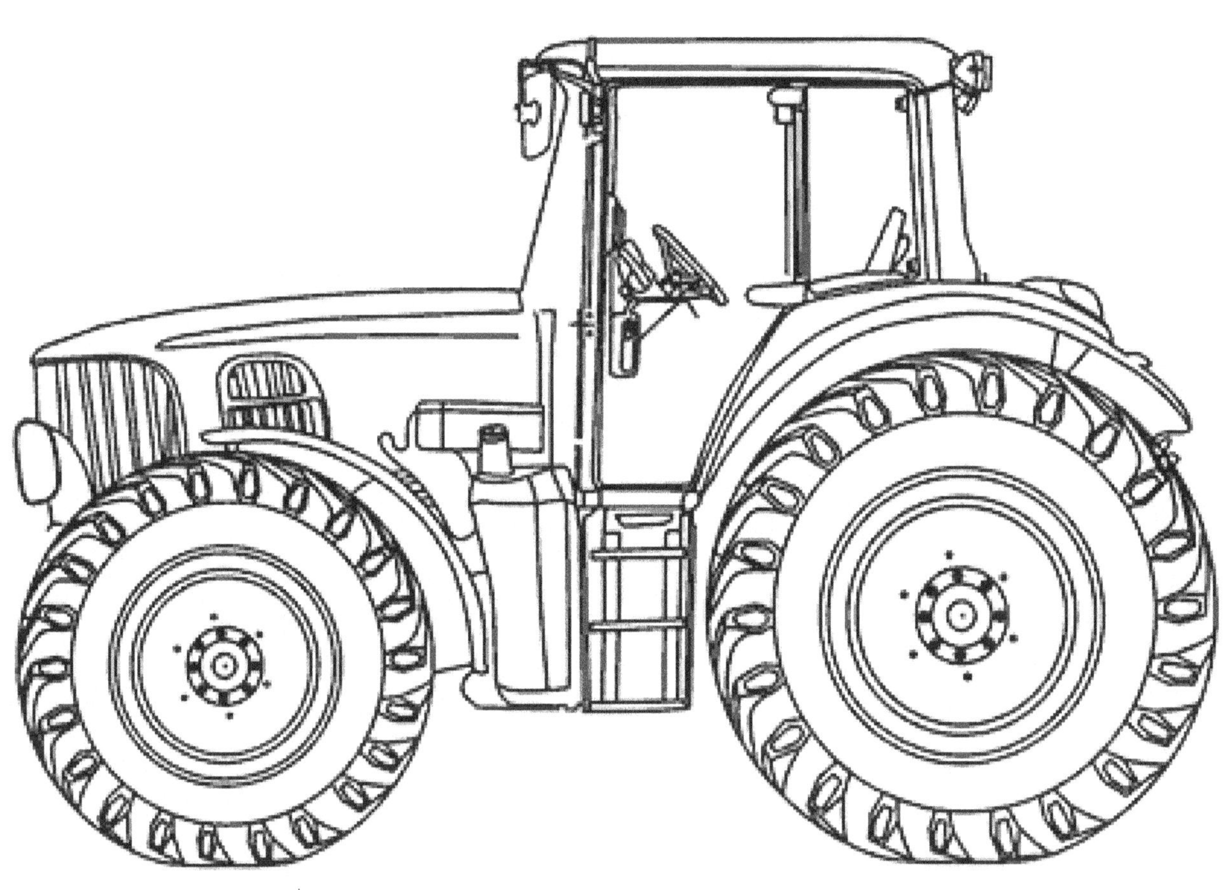

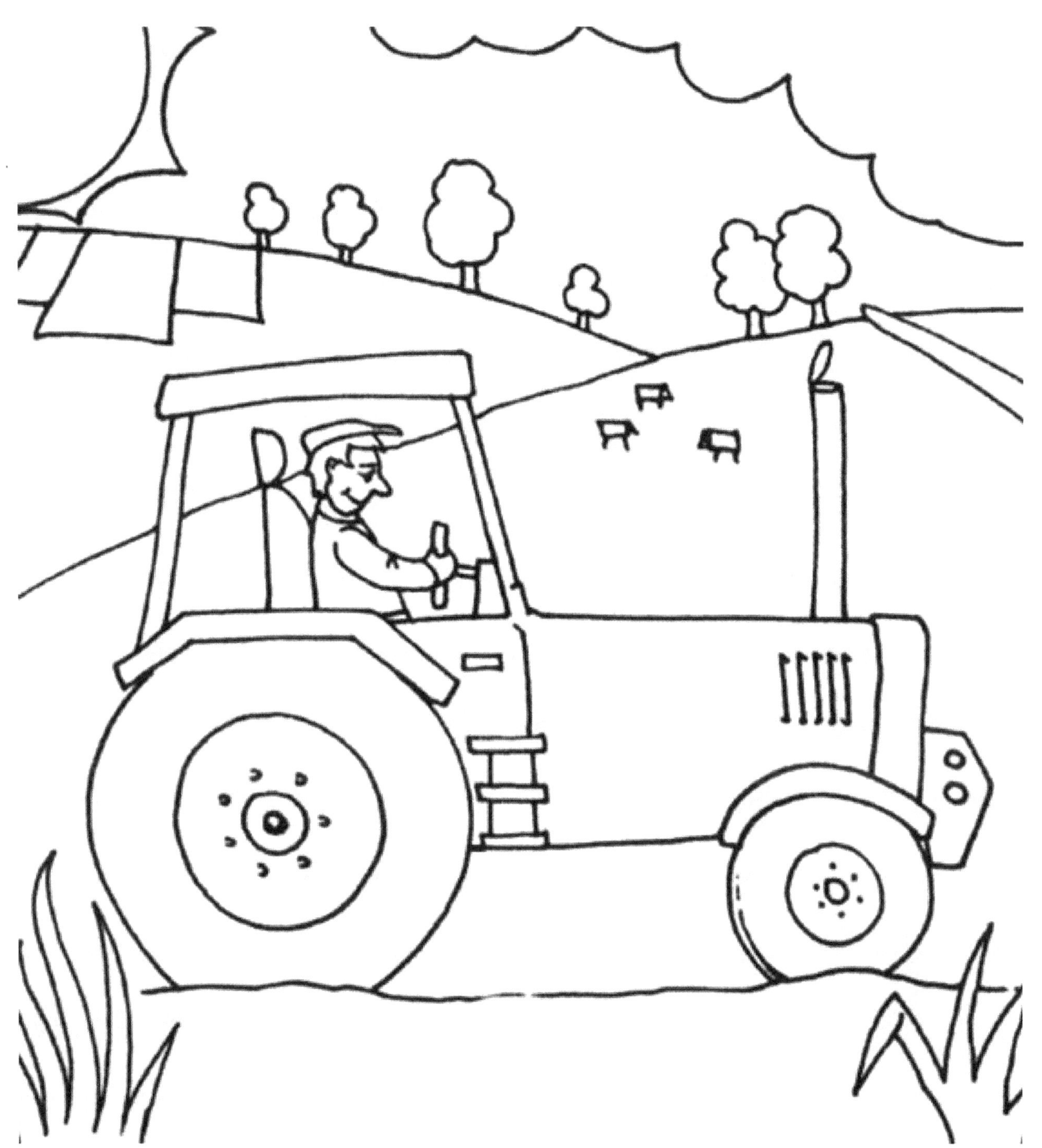

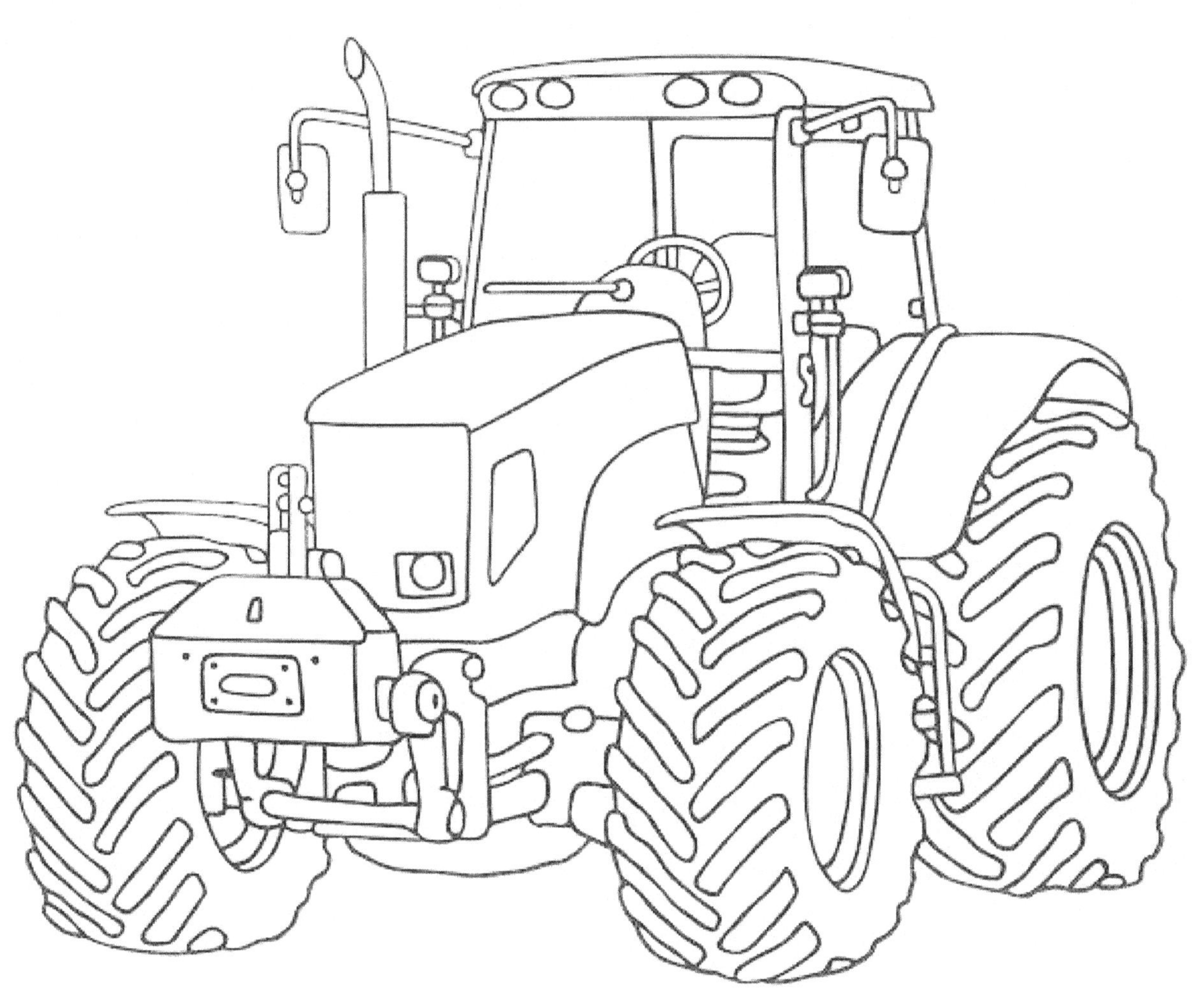

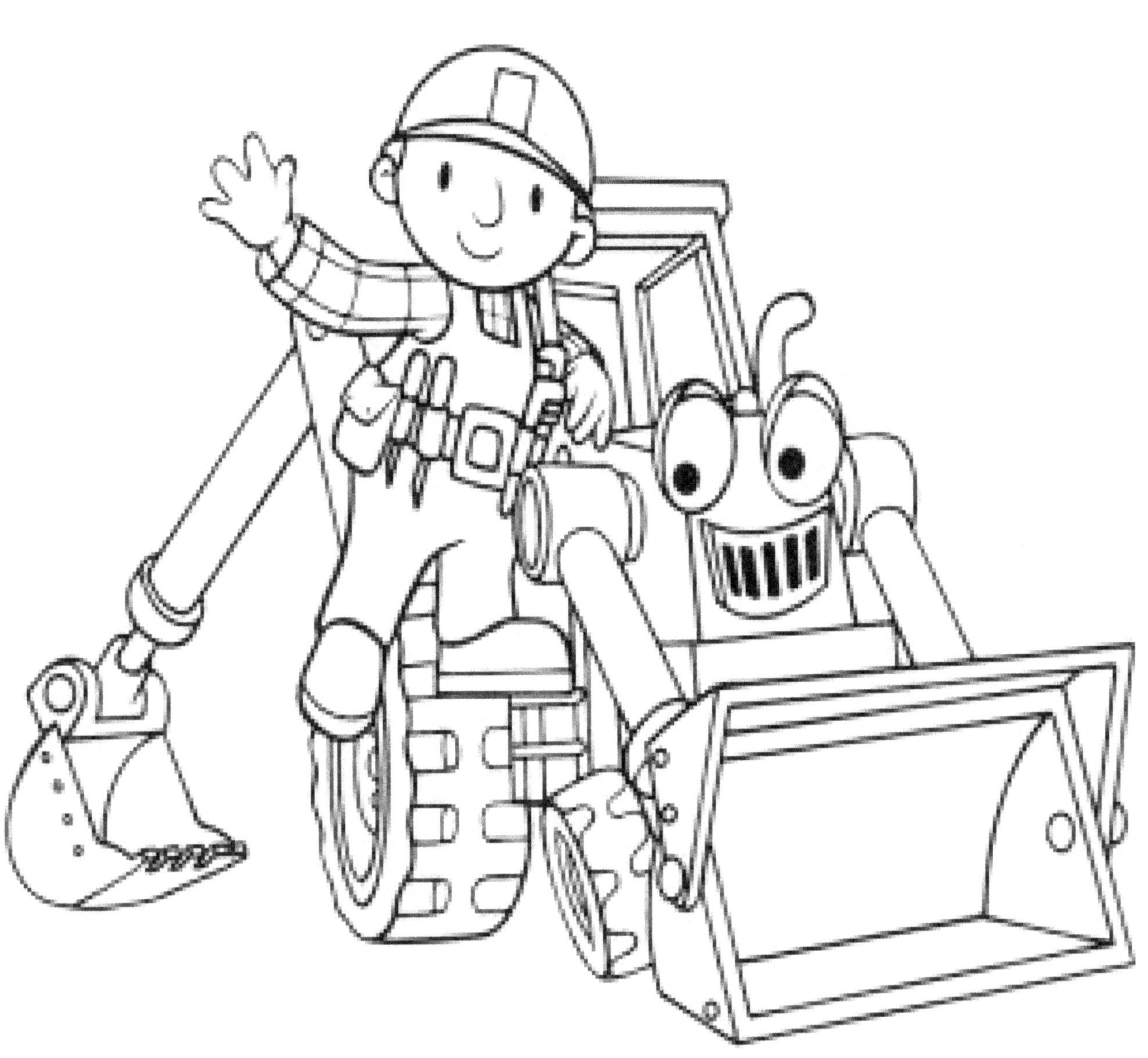

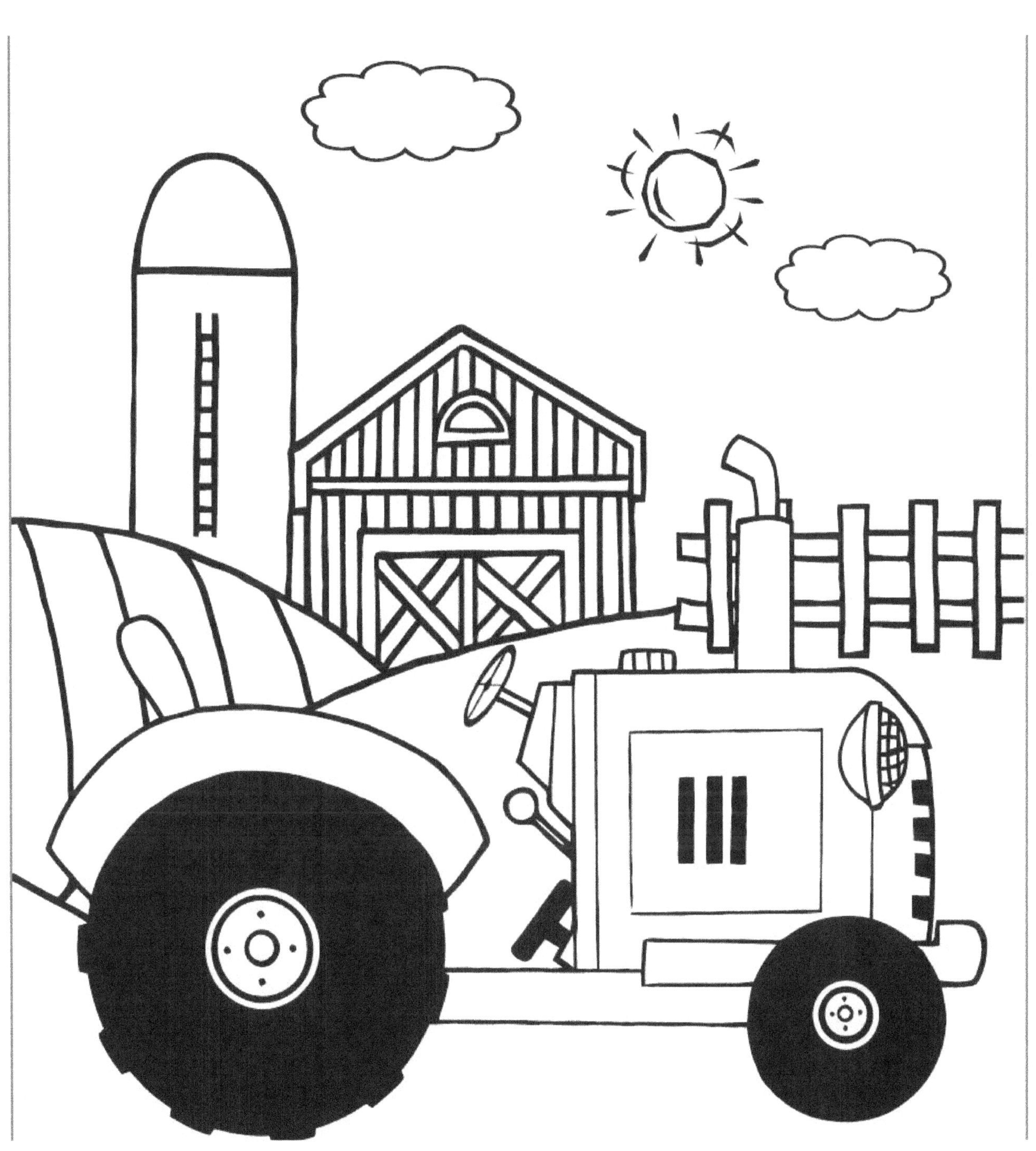

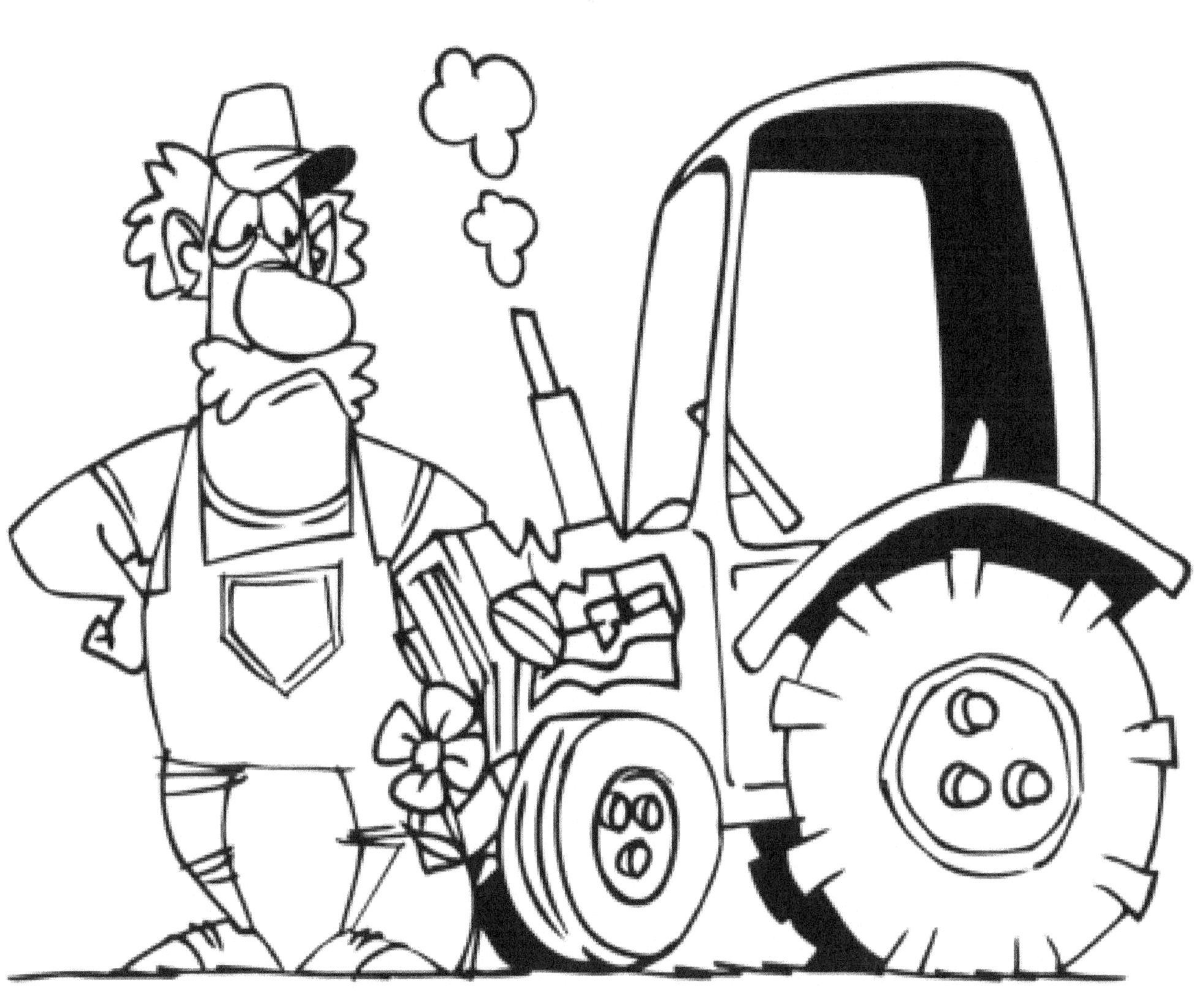

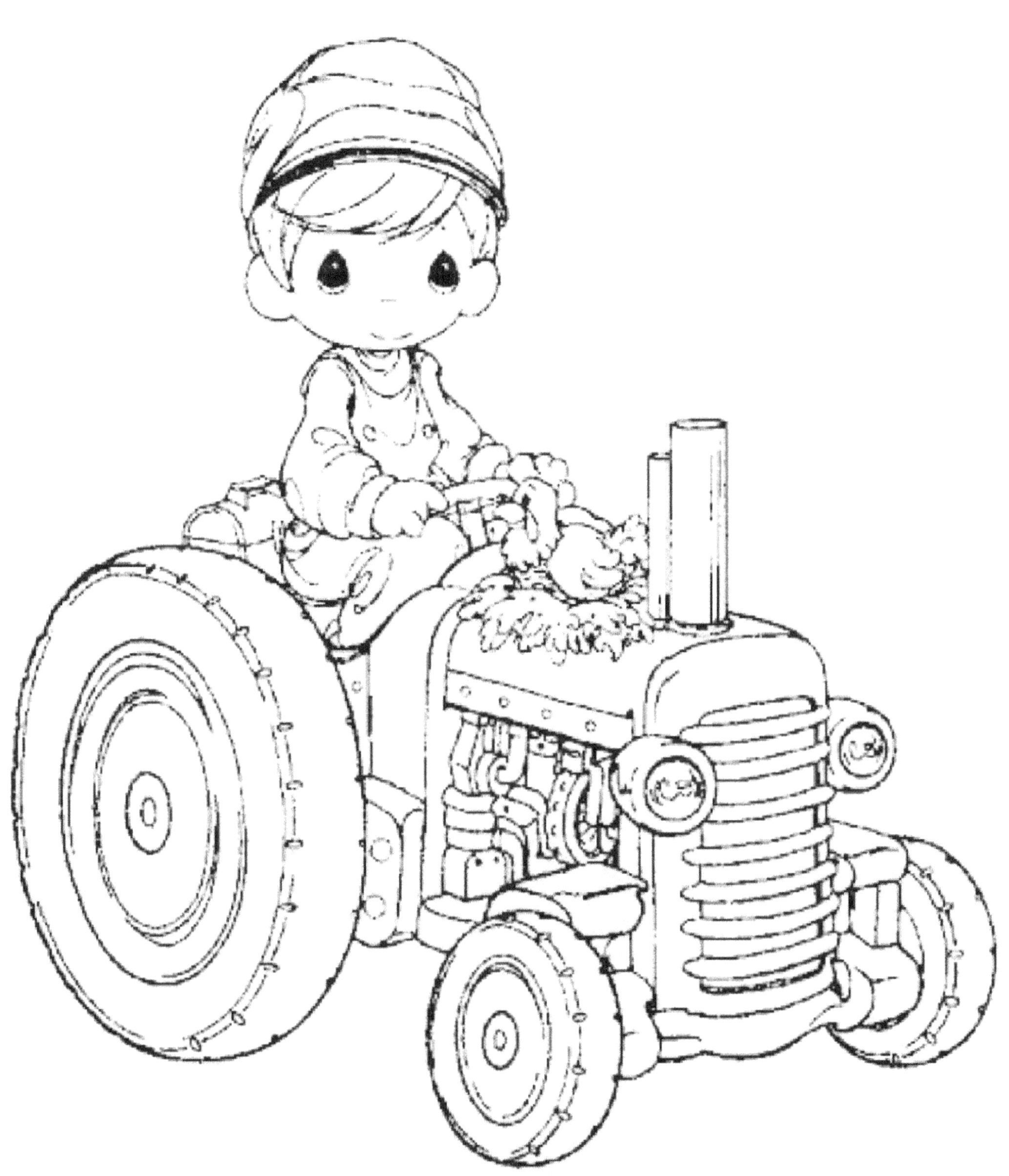

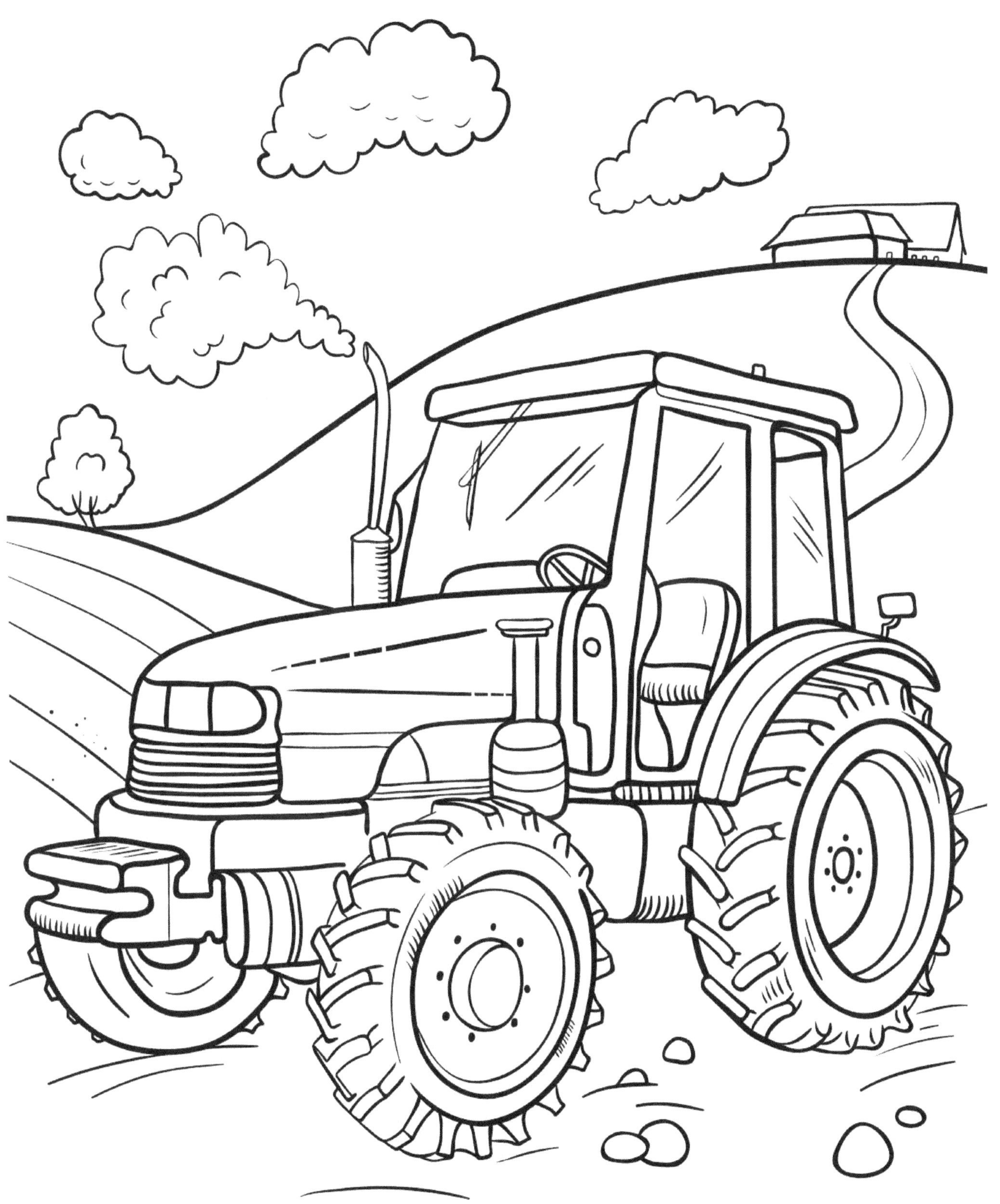

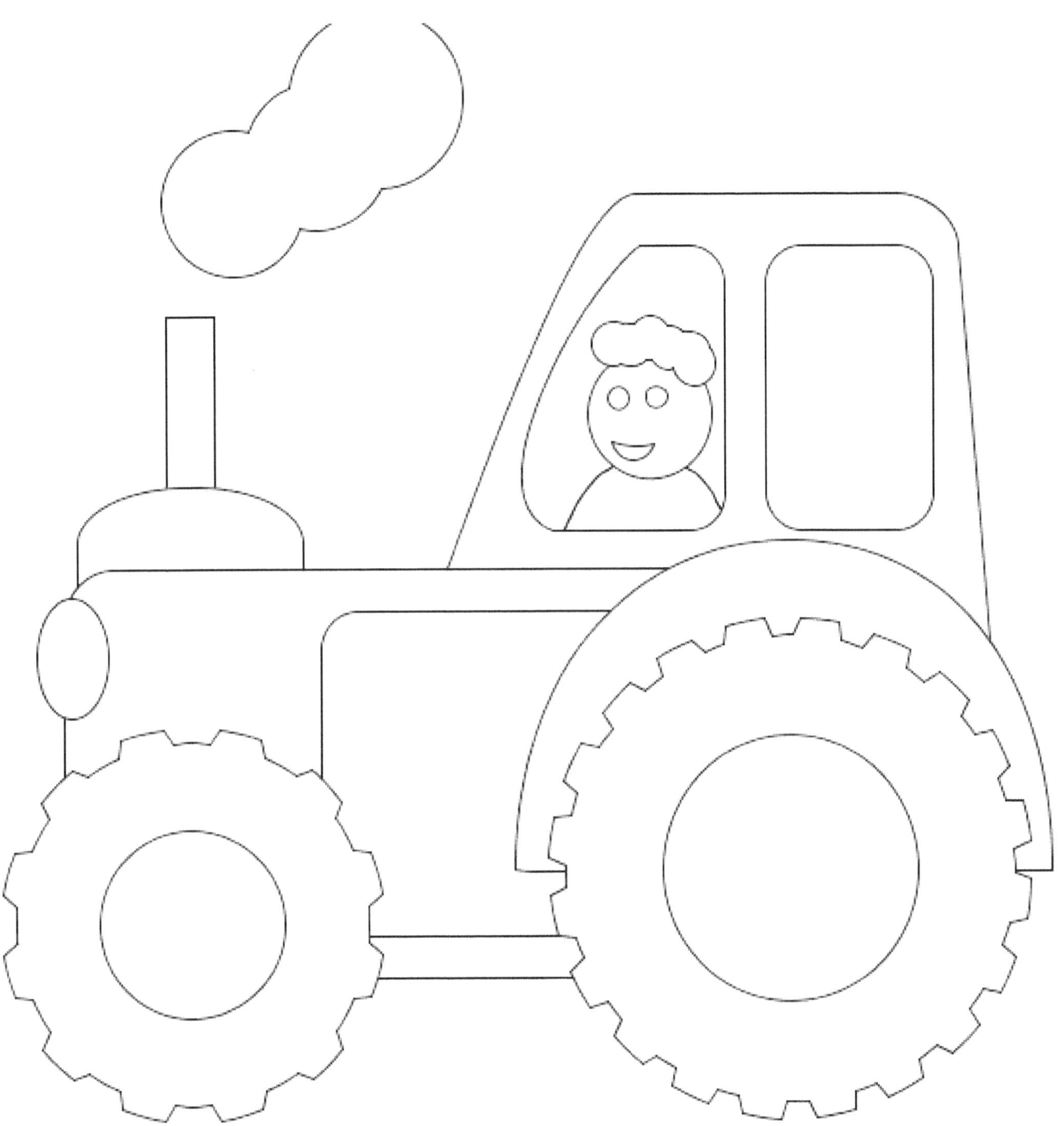

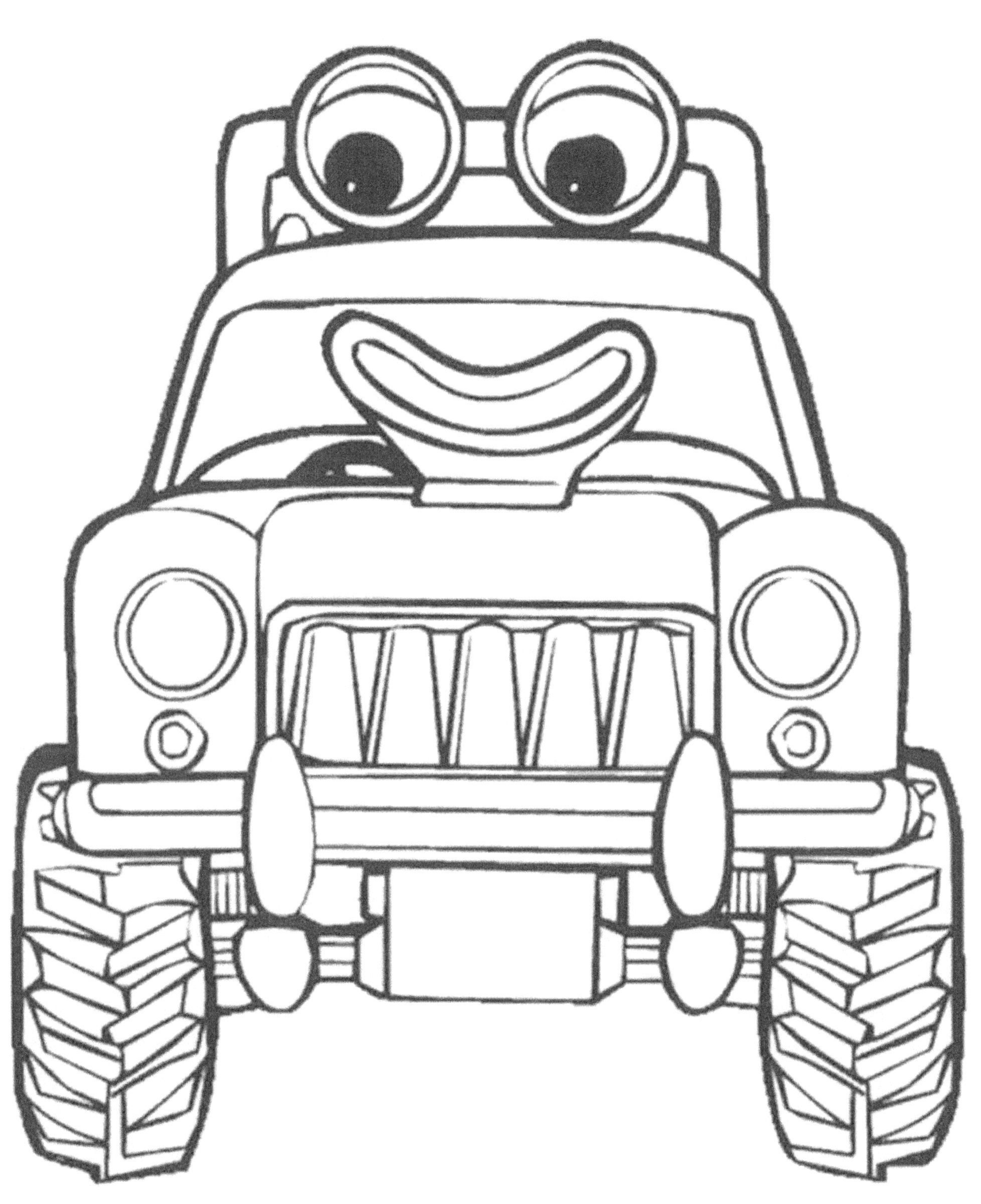

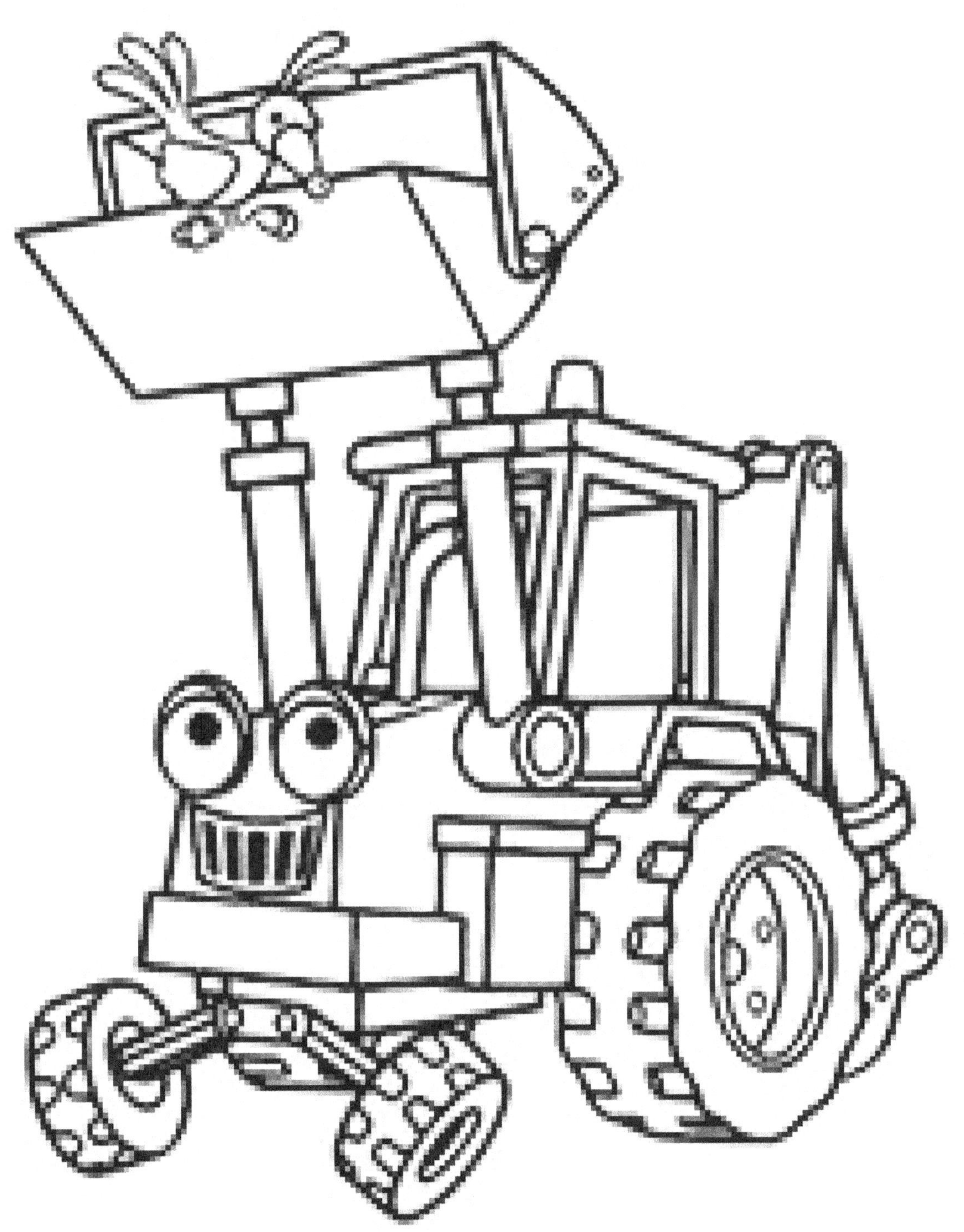

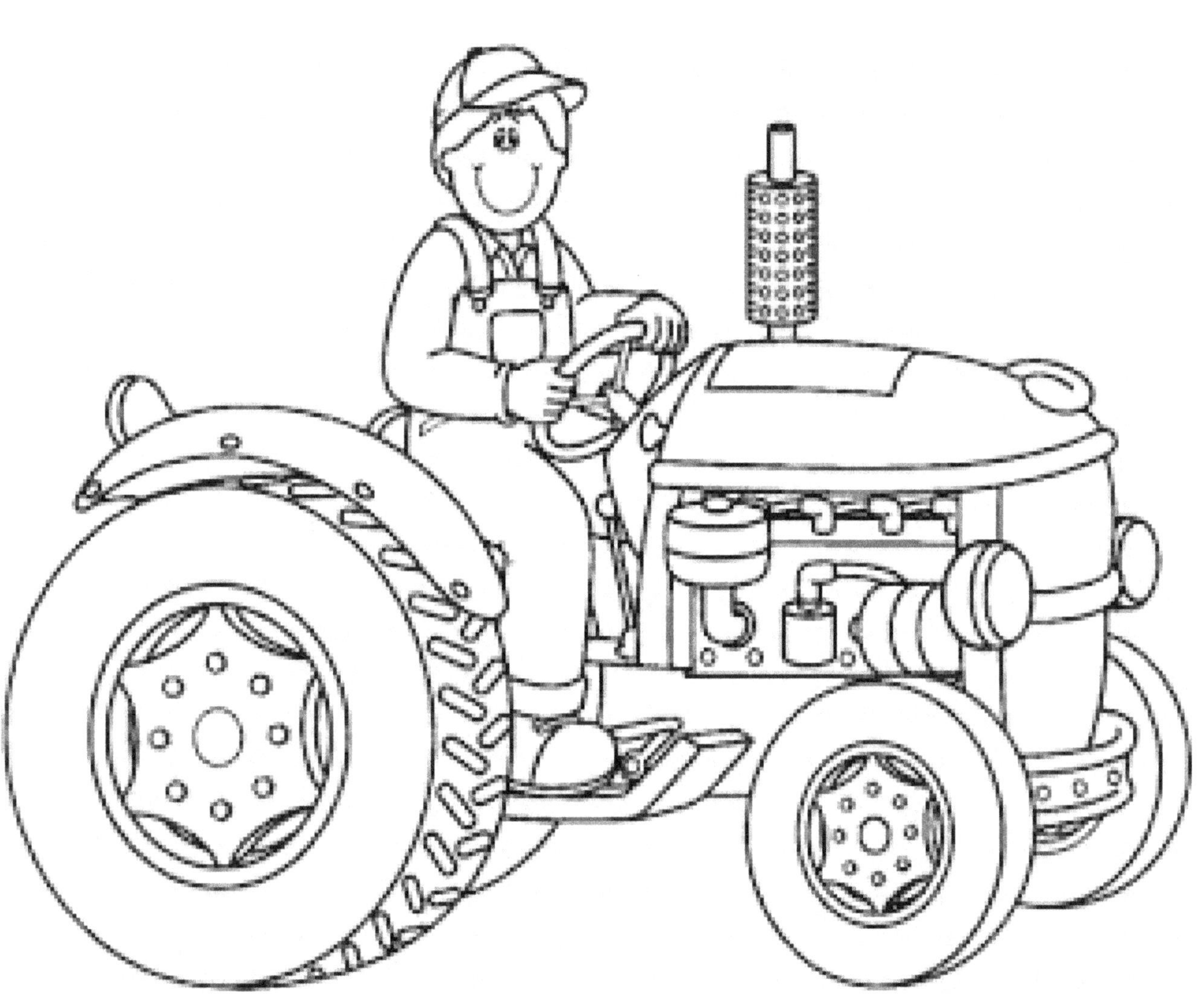

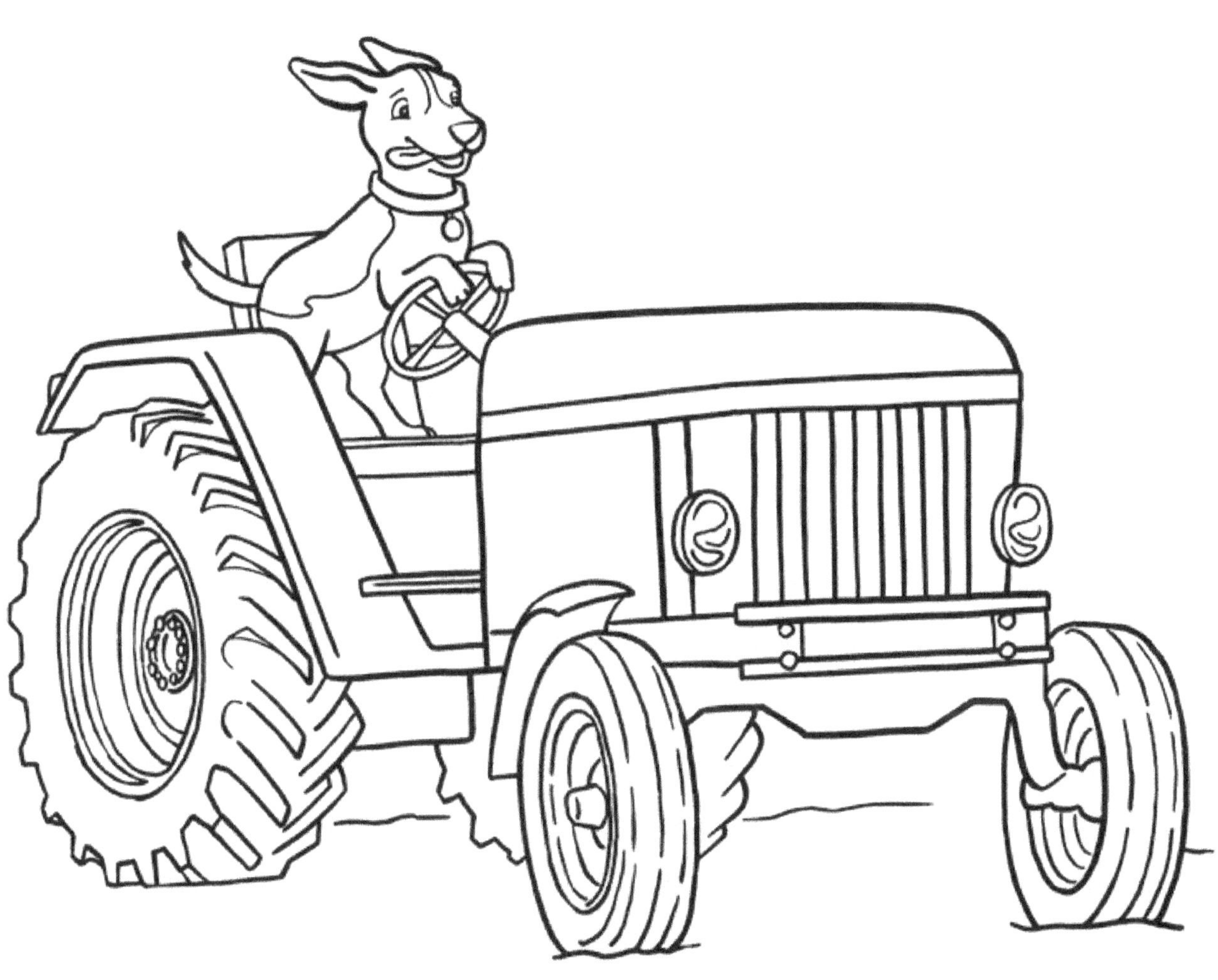

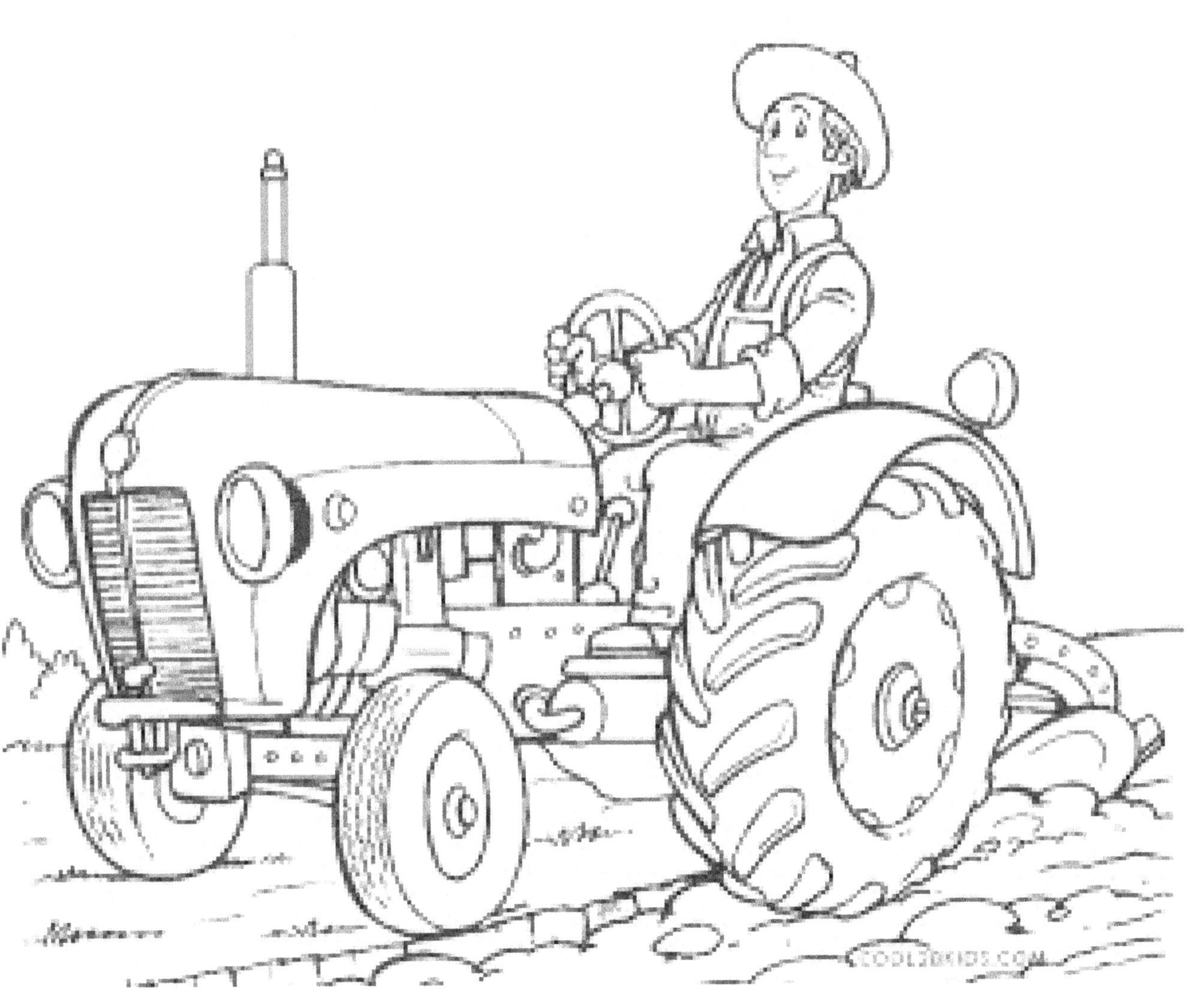

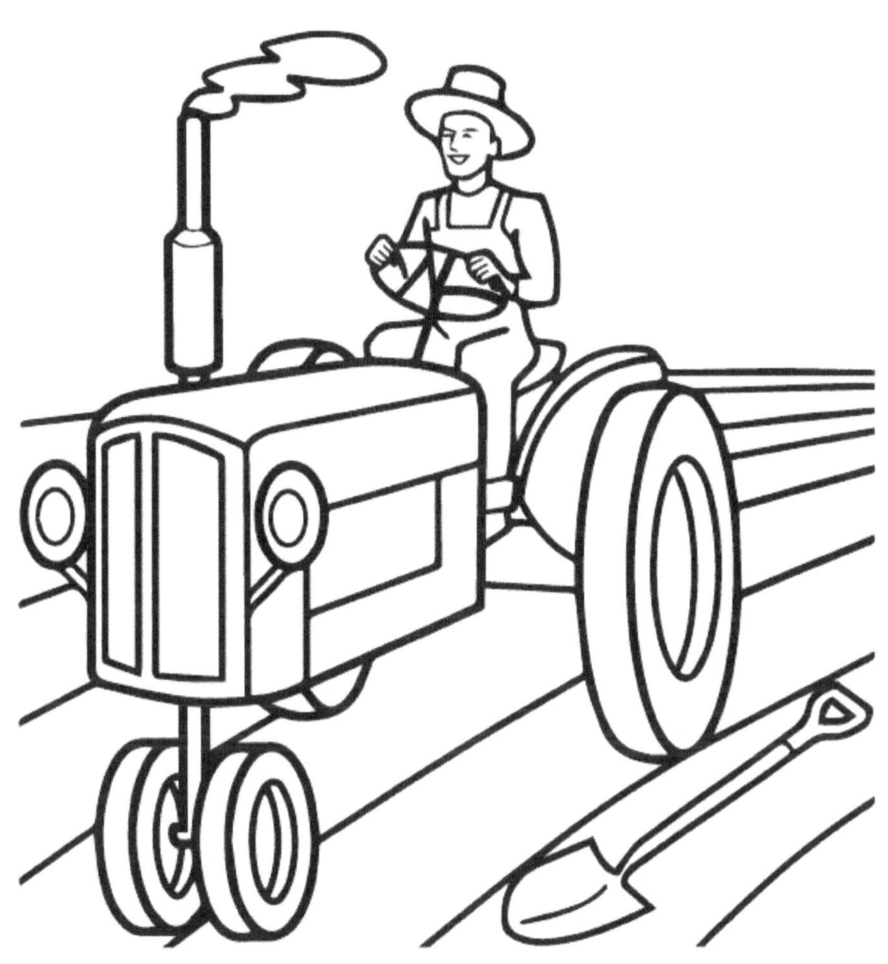

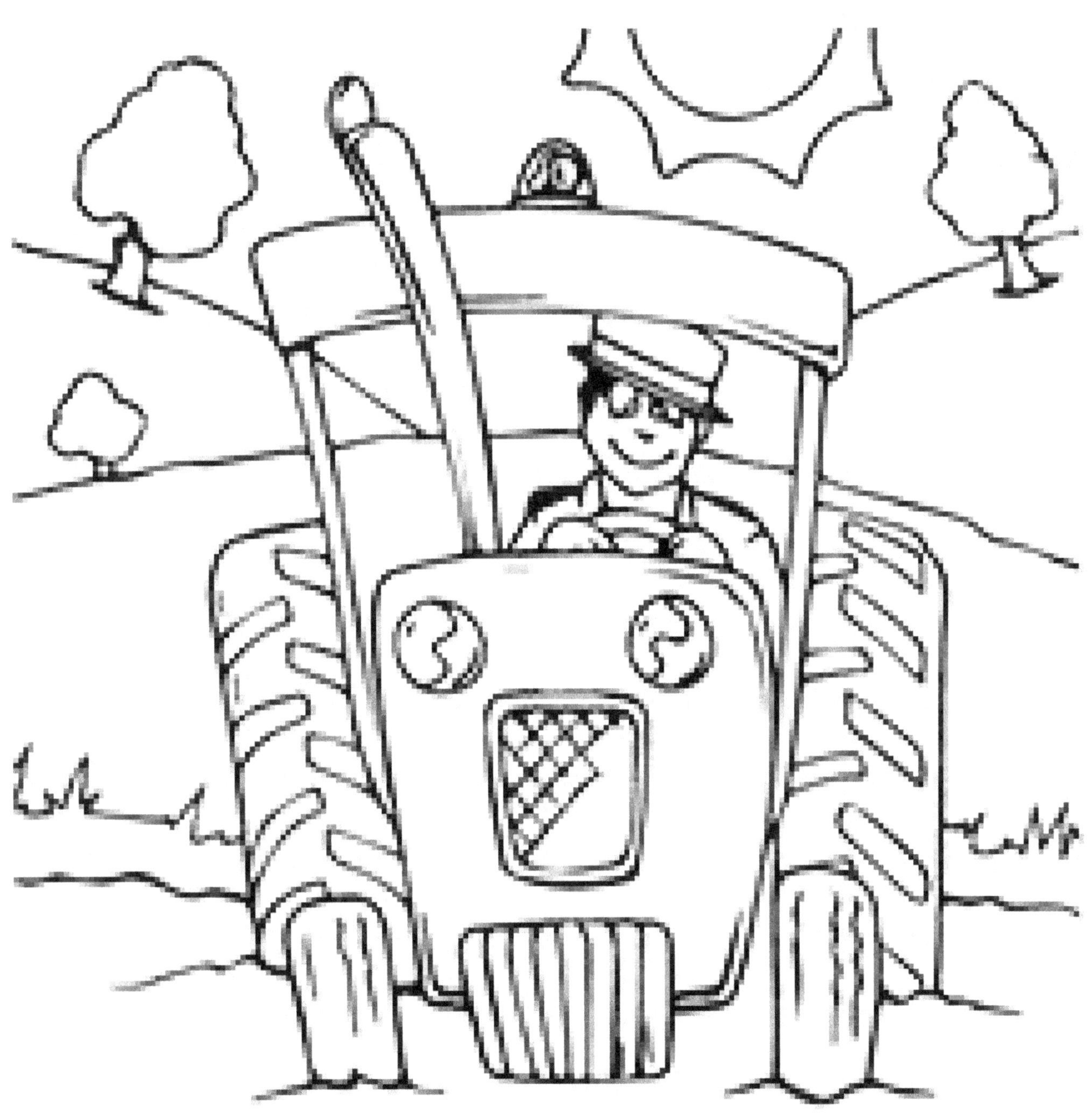

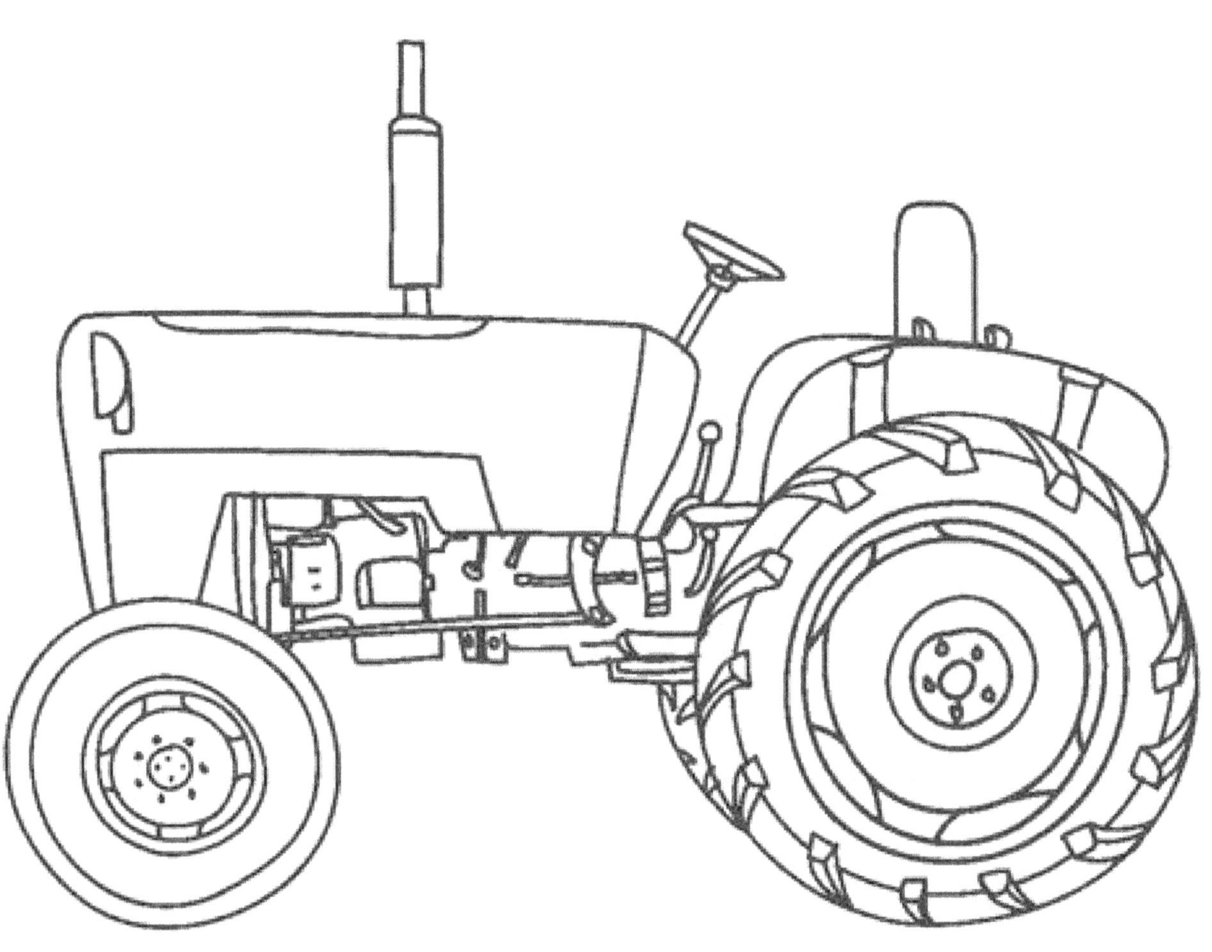

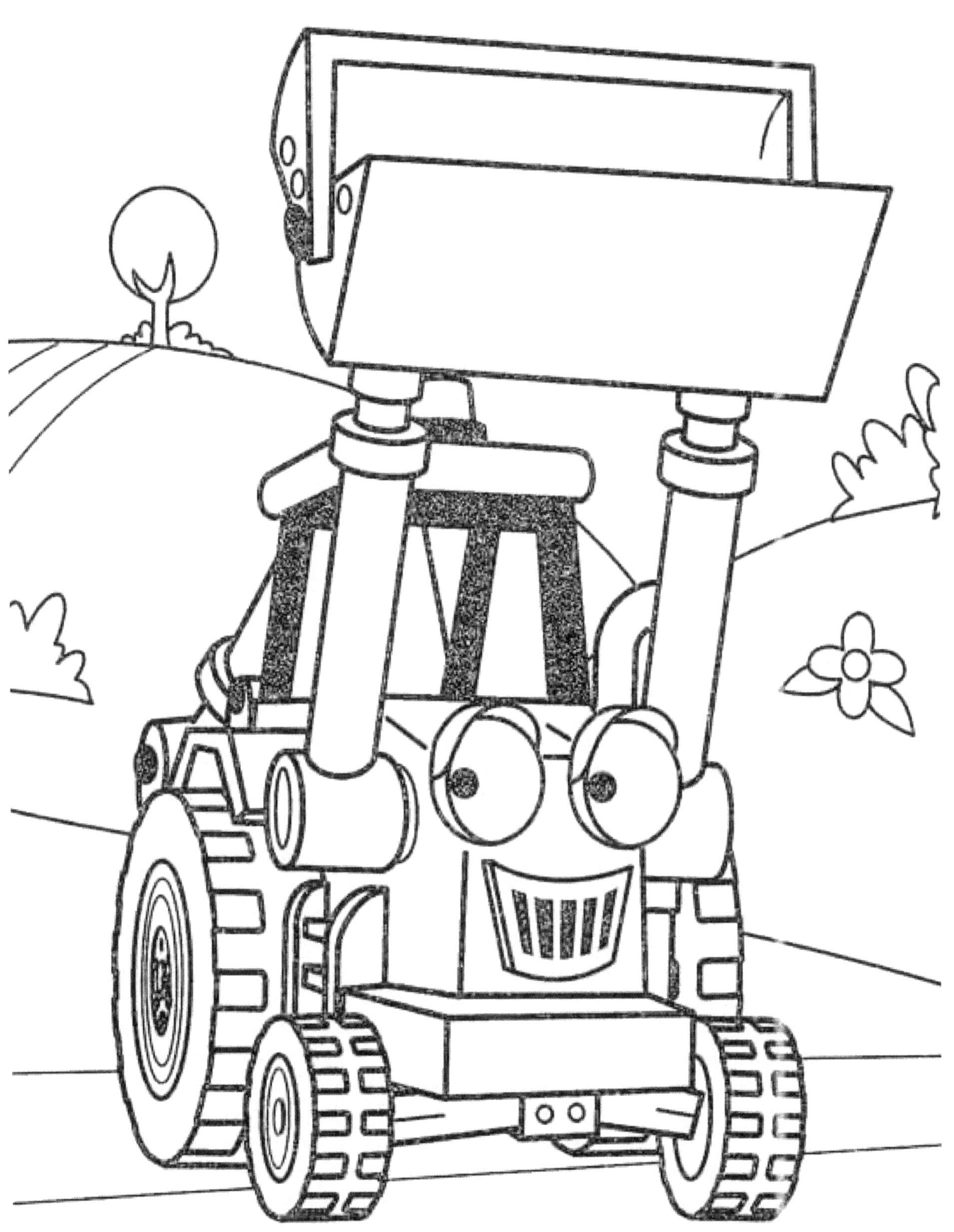